DATE DUE

D0672241

May 3 '72		
May 17 '72		
Jan 20 '73		
Apr 21 '73		
Dec 17 '73		
FEB 10 1975		
MAR 14 '77		
APR 27 '77		
5/24/78		
NOV 2 6 1980		
JUN 25 1981		
DEC. 2 6 1980		
DEC. 2 8 1982		
MAY 1 5 1989		
MAR 0 2		

27429

ILLINOIS POETS

A SELECTION

ILLINOIS POETS

A SELECTION

Edited by E. Earle Stibitz

Southern Illinois University Press *Carbondale and
Edwardsville*

Feffer & Simons, Inc. *London and Amsterdam*

PUBLICATION of this book has been made possible through a grant from Southern Illinois University as part of its contribution to the Illinois Sesquicentennial.

GRATEFUL ACKNOWLEDGMENT is made to the poets and publishers for their permission to reprint poems appearing in this volume.

GWENDOLYN BROOKS: "To Be in Love," "Riders to the Blood-Red Wrath," copyright © 1963 by Gwendolyn Brooks Blakely; "The Bean Eaters," copyright © 1959 by Gwendolyn Brooks; "The Lovers of the Poor," copyright © 1960 by Gwendolyn Brooks; from *Selected Poems* (1963) by Gwendolyn Brooks. Reprinted by permission of Harper & Row, Publishers.

PAUL CARROLL: "Chicago Elegy," from *Prairie Schooner*, XXXI (Fall 1957), © 1957 by the University of Nebraska Press; "Mother," first published in *The Paris Review*, Issue No. 34, Spring–Summer 1965; "Oriental Pastoral: Old Scholars, A Bird, A Plumtree," copyright, 1957, *The Western Review*. Reprinted by permission of publishers.

R. R. CUSCADEN: "Travel Poster," "The Crippled Girl," "The Dog Cemetery," from *Poems for a Ten Pound Sailfish and Other Sonnets* (The Elizabeth Press, 1963); "Derricks," "Northern Indiana, Sunday Afternoon," "Poet as Trumpet Player," "The First Death," from *Ups and Downs of a Third Baseman* (Firebird Imprints, Second Series, No. 1, 1963); reprinted by courtesy of the author. "Holiday," copyright 1965, *Chicago Review*, Vol. 17, 1964; reprinted by courtesy of the *Chicago Review*.

GEORGE DILLON: "Afternoon," "Pantomime for a Spring Twilight," "Twilight in a Tower," "Fall of Stars," "City of Wind," from *Boy in the Wind* by George Dillon, copyright 1927 by The Viking Press, Inc., 1955 by George Dillon; "September Moon," "The Summery Night Before the Frost," "The Hours of the Day," "The Dead Elm on the Hilltop," "This Dream is Strange," from *The Flowering Stone* by George Dillon, copyright 1931, © 1959 by George Dillon; reprinted by permission of The Viking Press, Inc.

GLENN WARD DRESBACH: "Cutting Weeds," "Deserted Farms," "To Wild Geese Over a Great City," from *Selected Poems* by Glenn Ward

Dresbach, copyright 1931 by Holt, Rinehart and Winston, Inc., copyright © 1959 by Glenn Ward Dresbach; reprinted by permission of Holt, Rinehart and Winston, Inc.; "A City Bridge in Snow," "Boy in a Coal Car," "A Lonely Field," from *The Collected (1914–1948) Poems of Glenn Dresbach*, The Caxton Printers, 1950; reprinted by permission of The Caxton Printers, Ltd.

EUGENE FIELD: "Human Nature," "A Patriot's Triumph," "Chicago Weather," "When Stedman Comes to Town," "Extinct Monsters," from *Poems of Eugene Field* (New York: Charles Scribner's Sons, 1949). Reprinted by courtesy of Charles Scribner's Sons.

ISABELLA GARDNER: "West of Childhood," "The Searchlight," "The Sloth," "Little Rock Arkansas," "Cowardice," "Abraham and Isaac," "Homo Gratia Artis," from *West of Childhood: Poems 1950–1965* by Isabella Gardner (copyright 1965 by Isabella Gardner Tate). Reprinted by permission of Houghton Mifflin Company.

JOHN HAY: "The Prairie," "Jim Bludso of the Prairie," "Banty Tim," from *The Complete Poetical Works of John Hay* (copyright 1913 by Clarence L. Hay). Reprinted by permission of Houghton Mifflin Company.

WILLIAM LEGGETT: "Lines Written on Leaving Illinois," "Address," from a copy of the Harris Collection of American Poetry and Plays, Brown University Library. Permission of Brown University Library to use manuscript copy of Leggett's *Poems*.

VACHEL LINDSAY: "The Illinois Village" (Part II, "A Gospel of Beauty"), "The Angel and The Clown," "Why I Voted the Socialist Ticket," reprinted with permission of The Macmillan Company from *Collected Poems* by Vachel Lindsay, copyright 1913 by The Macmillan Company; "Factory Windows are Always Broken," "Abraham Lincoln Walks at Midnight," reprinted with permission of The Macmillan Company from *Collected Poems* by Vachel Lindsay, copyright 1914 by The Macmillan Company, renewed 1942 by Elizabeth C. Lindsay; "Bryan, Bryan, Bryan, Bryan," reprinted with permission of The Macmillan Company from *Collected Poems* by Vachel Lindsay, copyright 1920 by The Macmillan Company, renewed 1948 by Elizabeth C. Lindsay; "The Eagle That Is Forgotten," reprinted with permission of The Macmillan Company from *Collected Poems* by Vachel Lindsay, copyright 1923 by The Macmillan Company, renewed 1951 by Elizabeth C. Lindsay; "Nancy Hanks, Mother of Abraham Lincoln," "The Flower-Fed Buffaloes," from *Going to the Stars* by Vachel Lindsay, copyright 1926 by D. Appleton & Company, renewed 1954 by Elizabeth C. Lindsay, reprinted by permission of Appleton-Century, affiliate of Meredith Press.

EDGAR LEE MASTERS: "The Hill," "Hod Putt," "Daisy Fraser," "Barney Hainsfeather," "Harry Wilmans," "Lucinda Matlock," "William H. Herndon," "Anne Rutledge," from *The Spoon River Anthology* (copyright 1914, 1915, 1942, by The Macmillan Company); "Chicago," from *Starved Rock* (copyright 1919, 1947, by The Macmillan Company); reprinted by permission of Ellen C. Masters. "Illinois Ozarks," from *Illinois Poems*, 1941; (copyright 1914 by Edgar Lee Masters). Reprinted by permission of Ellen C. Masters.

HARRIET MONROE: "The Columbian Ode," "Nancy Hanks," "A Power Plant," from *Chosen Poems: A Selection from My Books* by Harriet Monroe (copyright 1935 by The Macmillan Co.). Reprinted by permission of Marguerite F. Fletcher for the estate of Harriet Monroe.

WILLIAM VAUGHN MOODY: "An Ode in Time of Hesitation," "The Quarry," "On a Soldier Fallen in the Philippines," from *The Poems and Plays of William Vaughn Moody* (copyright 1912 by Harriet C. Moody). Reprinted by courtesy of Houghton Mifflin Company.

PAUL SCOTT MOWRER: "From Exile," "Wherever Bees," from *Poems Between Wars: Hail Illinois, France Farewell* by Paul Scott Mowrer (copyright 1941 by Paul Scott Mowrer); reprinted by permission of Paul Scott Mowrer. "Swarms," "After Rain," from *The Mothering Land—Selected Poems* (1918–1958) by Paul Scott Mowrer (copyright 1960 by Paul Scott Mowrer); reprinted by permission of Paul Scott Mowrer and The Golden Quill Press.

LISEL MUELLER: "On Finding a Bird's Bones in the Woods," "Cicadas," "Sunday Fishing," "Suspension Bridge: Twilight," "The People at the Party," "Ecology: the Lion," "The Lonesome Dream," from *Dependencies* by Lisel Mueller (copyright 1965 by the University of North Carolina Press); "The Gift of Fire," *Poetry, A Magazine of Verse*, July 1967. Reprinted by permission of the author and the publishers.

JOHN FREDERICK NIMS: "Girl Marcher," "Old Philosophy Professor," "Poetry Dignitary," from *Of Flesh and Bones* by John Frederick Nims (copyright 1967 by John Frederick Nims); reprinted by permission of Rutgers University Press. "Driving at Sunset," "The Weeds," "To Keep our Metaphysics Warm," from *A Fountain in Kentucky* by John Frederick Nims (copyright 1950 by John Frederick Nims); "Elevated," "City Rain at Midnight," from *The Iron Pastoral* by John Frederick Nims (copyright 1947 by John Frederick Nims); reprinted by permission of William Morrow and Company, Inc.

JESSICA NELSON NORTH: "Bogie," "Midway Sketches," "Spring Comes to Chicago," from *A Prayer Rug* by Jessica Nelson North (copyright 1923 by Will Ransom); "A Convent Walk," from *The Long Leash* by Jessica Nelson North (copyright 1928 by Jessica Nelson North); "The Mother," "Dinner Party," "Choreartium," "Apocalypse," from *Dinner Party* by Jessica Nelson North (copyright 1942 by Jessica Nelson North). Reprinted by courtesy of Jessica Nelson North.

ELDER OLSON: "Spring Ghost," "For the Demolition of a Theatre," "Jack-in-the-Box," "The Statue," "At a Military Ceremony," from *Collected Poems* by Elder Olson (copyright 1963 by Elder Olson); "Inscription for the Tomb of Man," from *Thing of Sorrow: Poems* by Elder Olson (copyright 1934 by Elder Olson). Reprinted by courtesy of Elder Olson.

HENRY RAGO: "A Roof-Top, Late August," "Abstraction," "Lovers That

Leave," from *The Travelers* by Henry Rago (copyright 1949 by Henry Rago; published by Golden Goose Press, 1949); reprinted by permission of the poet. "My Mother's Portrait," reprinted with permission of The Macmillan Company from *A Sky of Late Summer* by Henry Rago, © Henry Rago 1960; "Sit Now Quietly," reprinted with permission of The Macmillan Company from *A Sky of Late Summer* by Henry Rago, copyright 1952 by The Macmillan Company; "The Net" reprinted with permission of The Macmillan Company from *A Sky of Late Summer* by Henry Rago, © Henry Rago 1961.

CARL SANDBURG: "The Laughing Corn," "A Million Young Workmen," "Joliet," "Washerwoman," "Cool Tombs," from *Cornhuskers* by Carl Sandburg, copyright 1918 by Holt, Rinehart and Winston, Inc., copyright 1946 by Carl Sandburg; reprinted by permission of Holt, Rinehart and Winston, Inc. "Child of the Romans," "The Harbor," "A Fence," "Chicago," from *Chicago Poems* by Carl Sandburg, copyright 1916 by Holt, Rinehart and Winston, Inc., copyright 1944 by Carl Sandburg; reprinted by permission of Holt, Rinehart and Winston, Inc. "Crabapples," from *Good Morning, America* by Carl Sandburg, copyright 1928, 1956, by Carl Sandburg; reprinted by permission of Harcourt, Brace & World, Inc. "Letter S," "New Farm Tractor," "The Mayor of Gary," from *Smoke and Steel* by Carl Sandburg, copyright 1920 by Harcourt, Brace & World, Inc., copyright, 1948, by Carl Sandburg; reprinted by permission of Harcourt, Brace & World, Inc. "Peace Between Wars," "The Long Shadow of Lincoln: A Litany," from *Complete Poems* by Carl Sandburg, copyright, 1950, by Carl Sandburg; reprinted by permission of Harcourt, Brace & World, Inc. "The People, Yes," (Nos. 29, 57, 107) from *The People, Yes* by Carl Sandburg, copyright, 1936, by Harcourt, Brace & World, Inc., copyright 1964 by Carl Sandburg; reprinted by permission of the publisher, Harcourt, Brace & World, Inc.

MARJORIE ALLEN SEIFFERT: "The New Eden," "Dingy Street," "The Shop," "Pride," "Youth Visits our Inferno," from *The King with Three Faces and Other Poems,* by Marjorie Allen Seiffert (copyright 1929 by Charles Scribner's Sons). Reprinted by courtesy of Charles Scribner's Sons.

LUCIEN STRYK: "Bombardier," "A Sheaf for Chicago—Proem," "Words on a Windy Day," from *Notes for a Guidebook* by Lucien Stryk (Chicago: Swallow Press, Inc., 1965). Copyright © 1965 Lucien Stryk. Reprinted by permission of Swallow Press, Inc.

ROBERT SWARD: "In Cities," "Snow," "All the Mornings," "American Heritage," copyright © 1961, 1962, 1963, 1964, 1965, by Robert Sward. Reprinted by permission of the author from *Kissing the Dancer* and *Thousand-Year-Old Fiancee* (Ithaca, N. Y.: Cornell University Press).

BERT LESTON TAYLOR: "The Rime of the Clark Street Cable," "Miss Legion," "Reform in our Town," from "A Line-O'-Type or Two," *Chicago Daily Tribune,* 1911, by Bert Leston Taylor. Reprinted by courtesy of the *Chicago Tribune.*

EUNICE TIETJENS: "Transcontinental," "The Drug Clerk," "The Steam

Shovel," from *Body and Raiment* (copyright 1919 by Alfred A. Knopf);
"After War," Sonnet No. X "From the Mountains," from *Leaves in
Windy Weather* (copyright 1929 by Alfred A. Knopf; renewed, 1957,
by Cloyd Head). Reprinted by permission of Alfred A. Knopf. "Fire-
Brick," from *Poetry, A Magazine of Verse,* March 1940. Reprinted by
permission of *Poetry* and Cloyd Head for the estate of Eunice Tietjens.

MARK VAN DOREN: "Midland," "The Cornetist," "Family Prime," "Going
Home," "Bailey's Hands," "Defeated Farmer," "Culture of Corn,"
"Granary," "The Only World," "After Long Drought," from *Collected
and New Poems: 1924–1963* by Mark Van Doren, copyright © 1963
by Mark Van Doren. Reprinted by permission of Hill and Wang, Inc.

EDITH FRANKLIN WYATT: "A City Equinoctial," "Lake Winds," "To a City
Swallow," "City Vespers," from *The Wind in the Corn* (copyright 1917
by D. Appleton & Company). Reprinted by permission of Appleton-
Century, affiliate of Meredith Press.

Every effort has been made to trace the owners of copyright material used
in this book. Should any material have been included inadvertently with-
out the permission of the owner of the copyright, acknowledgment will
be made in any future edition.

For Ella

CONTENTS

III. NEW DIRECTIONS AND NEW CONVENTIONS, 1915–1940

IV. SOME CONTEMPORARIES, 1940–1968

INTRODUCTION

The quantitative fact that Illinois has reached its one hundred and fiftieth year is, by itself, a doubtful justification for publishing a book of Illinois poets. Nor is the validity of the undertaking made more certain by the artificial character of state boundaries in literary matters, though Illinois, substantially surrounded by Lake Michigan and the Wabash, Ohio, and Mississippi Rivers, is more naturally enclosed than most of the states. The 1968 Sesquicentennial, however, does provide an occasion and the stimulus for a retrospective examination of the one hundred and fifty years to see what of poetic concern has happened in this region—or, more accurately, this section of a region—of the country as a whole. To say "of the country as a whole" is to suggest the main literary interest of such an examination as this book reflects, for we have arrived, surely, at a stage of intellectual development in which state pride has become a decidedly minor element in cultural concerns.

Throughout the compiling of this anthology, therefore, the attempt has been made to examine the work of those who can be called Illinois poets with an eye to selecting poems that not only embody characteristics of the section but also have a meaningful relationship—partly because of those very characteristics—to American literature as a whole. It is indeed possible that in the sectional context an acquaintance with the poetry presented here, both that which has continued to be read and that which has been historically forgotten, may result in qualified insights into the nature of our literature and our literary history nationally considered. This is the hope, even though in an anthology of this kind with its minimal comment suggestions of such insights must remain largely implicit.

In the relationship of the state region to the national whole, it is significant that during much of its history Illinois consisted, for a time, of frontier country and, more lastingly, of recent frontier country. In comparison with the literarily dominant East, it was a relatively open land, economically and culturally. The East from the beginning of its literary productiveness experienced a comparative density of population, the early rise of cities, an industrial development, and the advent of specialization, all of which, even if seemingly little compared with what comes later, indicate a link with present urbanization. This eastern development took place too early and too rapidly for the literature to record the impact clearly. Again by contrast, the Midwest, including Illinois with its continuing rural and less confined culture, experienced its urbanization later and more slowly than the East. Thus Illinois writing, of which the poetry in this volume is representative, can offer both a unique historical picture of a section of American civilization and literature, and a slow-motioned one of what essentially took place in the civilization and literature of the older part of the nation. Even today, Illinois as a part of Mid-America retains to some degree attitudes reflective of its more open country, not least of which is a somewhat optimistic and even romantic spirit; yet one needs to underscore *"to some degree,"* for Illinois like every section of America is rapidly becoming an integral part of a total urban culture.

The choice of poems for this volume has been directly conditioned by the view of Illinois as part of the Midwest. Thus the effort has been made to include, as consistently as possible, not just poetry by Illinois poets but poetry that also is in some way Illinoisan or midwestern in subject matter and spirit, assuming rather boldly that this last is in someway identifiable. As the concern has been, at the same time, to make the selection representative of successive periods in Illinois history, the collection as a whole reflects substantially the poetic development in the state. On an objective or topic level, this approach has meant the inclusion of poems about the Illinois region— the prairies, the lingering pastoral or rural country, the village, the developing mechanization, and, on occasion, social or political events and persons. This partial list may again suggest what is perhaps the rather special character of Illinois: its having had within its borders some of the most rural parts of America and at the same time some of the most truly urban, particularly the metropolitan area of Chicago —not always disparately, for the rural is present in the city and the city is discoverable in the countryside. The mention of Chicago calls to mind what to some readers may be an interesting facet of the present collection, the appearance of some twenty poems which have that city as their central subject. It may be appropriately noted, too, that there is a considerable gathering of poems—a dozen or so—about Lincoln, another "Illinois subject."

On a more genuinely poetic or subjective level, a comparable effort has been made to include Illinois poetry, poetry that reflects the section in attitude and feeling. Revealed in the subjective expression concerning the land, war, Lincoln, the city, labor, and other subjects, the spirit of these poems ranges from the pastoral and idealistic and romantic to the relatively realistic and even pessimistic. Admittedly the selection of poetry on such a preconceived basis creates a danger that the quality of a poem as a poem will be subordinated to its representativeness; and this, in turn, may mean that a given poet is unfairly represented by something less than his best. Though I have been conscious of this danger, I know that it has not been altogether avoided; one confronts here the almost inevitable weakness of a thematic anthology. On the other hand, it can be fairly said that in Illinois poetic history poems involving the time and the place are often superior to those consciously seeking to be more universal. Also it should be indicated that although the Illinois principle of selection has been operative throughout, its application becomes less tenable, and so has been modified, in the choice of poetry of more recent times when both the increased maturity of the poetry and the decline of sectionalism are evident.

A central question, it will be noted, remains unanswered: what is an Illinois poet? It is a question that cannot be answered in a manner satisfactory to every reader, and all that can be done, or really needs to be done, is to make clear the view that has guided the present choice of poets. Although in the consideration of each "candidate" there has been an initial concern with Illinois birth, residence, and education, these matters have been less decisive than the fact that the poet has had a significant, generally his most significant, poetic connection with the state. The specific application of this requirement, of course, has involved judgments. It may be, for example, that I have included a poet who wrote in Illinois and moved on to other connections, whereas another compiler would not have included him. And so with other variations in the application of this view. When doubts about the Illinois credentials of a given poet have persisted, the decision has been made on the basis of the poetry itself, using the Illinois principle of selection already discussed. Certain other a priori requirements have been operative as well: for one thing, a writer to have been considered must be known mainly as a poet—for example, Sherwood Anderson, though writing relevant poetry, has not been included; again, it has seemed desirable that a substantial body of the poet's published work be available for consideration. Quality judgments, of course, have been made. Although the level of poetry in a historical and sectional anthology such as this will not be as consistently high as in a general collection of American poetry, still numerous poets—especially those of the earlier years—have been excluded on the basis of literary value-judgments. Obviously the likes and dislikes of the person choosing the poetry are reflected; still on the grounds indicated I have included poems that I do not particularly care for. Even with the varied restrictions, a goodly number of poets and even more poems were eligible than the size of the volume would allow if most of the poets chosen were to be represented by more than a very few poems. Unfortunately, certain poets and poems have had to be passed by because of copyright difficulties. If then, the reader discovers omissions with which he disagrees, the reason may lie with one or more of the requirements indicated—or, conceivably, with just plain oversight.

The selections are presented in four sections, each marking not only a chronological period but also, on the basis of the character of the poetry within the section, a stage in the development of Illinois poetry from the beginnings of the state to the present. Within the sections, the poets and the poetry are arranged in a loose time order, and the writings of each poet are grouped as far as is feasible by subject or concern. The four divisions are: I. "Some Beginnings," 1818–1880; II. "Turnings," 1880–1915; III. "New Directions and New Conventions," 1915–1940; and IV. "Some Contemporaries," 1940–1968. The dates given represent a somewhat arbitrary designation of periods in the poetic development mentioned above and do not necessarily mean that within a given section poems are included that were written immediately after the initial year or right up to the terminal date.

In a substantial way this book is the result of a collaboration, and I am happy to try to recall and to record here the many individuals and institutions that have aided in its making. To all of these must go a large share of the credit for whatever virtues this anthology possesses; whatever failures that it must admit to are basically of my own creation. My apologies are offered to any that I inadvertently fail to mention and also to those whose advice I might have more effectively followed.

High on the list of "collaborators" are Professor Alan M. Cohn, head of the Humanities Division of the Morris Library at Southern Illinois University, and Miss Kathleen Eads and others of this division who throughout have assisted in many ways. My thanks are extended to other members of the staff of this library: to Mr. Ralph Bushee and his assistants in the Rare Book Room for a variety of help, to Mrs. Maxine Walker for her handling of inter-library loans, and to Professor Hensley C. Woodbridge for valuable bibliographical suggestions. Also for important help bibliographically I would thank Mr. Clyde Walton and the Illinois State Historical Society at Springfield. I record, too, my genuine appreciation of the aid given by the many staff members, here unnamed, of the libraries in which I was privileged to work: the Newberry Library, the Library of the Chicago Historical Society, the University of Chicago and the University of Illinois Libraries, and the Dayton and the Chicago Public Libraries. I wish particularly to thank Mrs. Pamela Mason of the "Harriet Monroe Modern Poetry Collection" in the University of Chicago Library for her patient work in providing a number of hard-to-find items. Other libraries throughout the country were of great assistance in their generous lending of needed materials: the Library of Congress and the university libraries at Brown, Princeton, Ohio State, Illinois, and California at Los Angeles. Special mention should be made of the Union Catalogue Division of the Library of Congress for its help in locating many sought-for books.

For valuable suggestions about the present undertaking as a whole I thank Mr. Henry Rago of *Poetry* magazine. My sincere thanks go to the Department of English and the College of Liberal Arts and Sciences at Southern for the grant of research time that greatly facilitated my work. Finally, I would express at this time my deep gratitude for the gracious assistance in this task, as in many others, of the late Professor Robert D. Faner, for many years a member and in recent years chairman of the Department of English at this University, whose sudden death in December, 1967, has intensified the awareness of his generosity and friendship.

Carbondale, Illinois
January, 1968   *E. Earle Stibitz*

1. SOME BEGINNINGS

AS IT IS quite speculative to identify the Illinois authorship of the earliest balladry and newspaper verse in the pre-state Illinois region, it has seemed best to begin with examples of verse published in Illinois after it became a state in 1818. To most present day readers, this early publishing activity will seem to have taken place in rather unlikely locations, for it is not generally remembered that the settlement and growth of Illinois was chiefly from the southeast and south. Such places as Shawneetown, Kaskaskia, Vandalia, and Edwardsville were the governmental and cultural centers of greatest importance in these years. For example, it was in 1830 at Vandalia, then capital of Illinois, that James Hall, a lawyer much interested in literary matters, established *The Illinois Monthly Magazine,* the first literary journal in the state. By contrast the northern area's first comparable, but inferior magazine, *The Gem of the Prairie,* of Chicago, was not begun until 1844; in fact, it was not until 1833 that the small settlement of Fort Dearborn was incorporated as the town of Chicago.

"Some Beginnings" seeks through a limited number of samples to represent the verse effort of the first half century or so of the state's history; and, at the same time, it seeks to make evident the dual beginnings—that in the southern part and that in the northern. The dual aspect is most neatly demonstrated by representing, on the one hand, Illinois' first book of verse, that by William Leggett, published in 1822 at Edwardsville, and, on the other, by including selections from William Kenyon's *Miscellaneous Poems,* published in Chicago in 1845 (at times mistakenly referred to as the first book of verse in the state). I use the term *verse* advisedly as being more applicable than *poetry,* but even though the poetic quality of the verse written during these years in Illinois does leave much to be desired, it is of some literary historical interest to see what were the necessary beginnings toward poetry.

William Leggett, the first writer to be represented in this section, came from the East to Illionis when he was about eighteen, and after a few years in Edwardsville left to join the navy. He later became fairly well known in journalism and was an assistant editor on the New York *Evening Post* under William Cullen Bryant. Micah P. Flint was the son of Timothy Flint, frontier preacher and author of various works, including *Recollections of Ten Years in the Mississippi Valley,* in which 1826 volume the Cahokia poem by Micah appeared when he was nineteen. "The Silent Monks" was also a youthful effort, for Flint died in 1830. James Hall, who was active as an editor-writer in Shawneetown before going to Vandalia, was not only a writer of verse but also the author of *Letters From the West* (1828) and of various stories and sketches. John H. Bryant had an important family literary connection as the brother of William Cullen Bryant, in light of which relationship it is of interest to note the points of similarity between the 1831 "Sketch," given here, and William Cullen's "Inscription for an Entrance to a Wood" of 1815. John Bryant arrived in Illinois in 1831 and settled as a farmer near Princeton, where he lived out a long life. William Kenyon came to Chicago as a young lawyer from the East and settled in Naperville. In the preface to *Miscellaneous Poems* he says his poems "have spontaneously sprung and blossomed on the prairie." Benjamin Stribling of Virginia, Illinois, makes his sole and perhaps less than overwhelming claim to literary remembrance with the volume of verse represented here. John Hay, secretary to Lincoln, and Secretary of State, as well as writer, had a relatively short but significant connection with Illinois. The Pike County of the *Ballads* is situated along the Mississippi in southwestern Illinois. The remaining writers —M. H. Jenks, Josephine Bassett, Mrs. Wiltse, and Thomas Chard— are included for the Illinois character of their verse and as representative of the magazine "poetry" of the day, rather than for their documentable biographical connections with Illinois or the high quality of their writing.

WILLIAM LEGGETT

Lines Written on Leaving Illinois, Aug. 29, 1822 *

would not one suffice?
Thy shaft flew thrice, and thrice my peace was slain.
Night Thoughts.

I Did not think to leave this land
    Would cost one pang, a single sigh,
But while I wave my parting hand,
    Tears, burning tears, suffuse my eye.

'Twas here I follow'd to the tomb,
    With breaking heart, two sisters dear;
Eliza,† too, in youthful bloom,
    Was snatch'd away and buried here.

Beneath the prairie turf they lie,
    And sweetest wild-flow'rs deck the sod;
Their spirits soar beyond the sky
    In sweet communion with their God.

But still the tear of deep regret
    To worth like theirs must e'er be given,
Affection mourns their absence yet,
    Tho' angels now, they dwell in heaven.

---

* The two poems by Leggett given here are from his *Poems* ("Edwardsville: Printed by and for the author, 1822"). The only known extant copy of *Poems* is in the Brown University Library. The present poems are as they appear in a manuscript copy of the book made by William Gowans in 1863, which copy is also in the Brown University Library. In Part I some obvious errors in the original printing of the poems have been corrected, and a few changes in punctuation have been made for the purpose of clarity.

† In a later volume of poems, *Leisure Hours From Sea* (1825), Eliza is the "lady" in "Lines on the Death of a Young Lady who was Drowned in the Ohio River," a poem which is poetically even more dubious than the present one.

3

Address

Written at the request of the preceptress of the St. Louis Academy, for one of the young ladies under her tuition to deliver, at an examination.

> *The world was sad—the garden was a wild—*
> *And man the hermit sigh'd—till woman smiled.*
> CAMPBELL

Why all this anxious tumult in my breast?
Be firm my heart!—rain throbbings sink to rest!
No envious tribe, with bitter taunt and sneer,
But only friends, approving friends, are here,
Who, unrestrain'd by critics' nicer laws,
Will pay our efforts with their warm applause.

Kindred and friend, I'm hither sent to ask
Your kind indulgence on our evening task.
No vet'rains we, who, with unchanging face,
Can meet the terrors of a public place;
But blushing maidens, who have come to tell
What fruits we've pluck'd in Learning's mazy dell. —

And should the falt'ring voice, the timid mien,
Betray the war our feelings wage within
Oh! Then remember that the female heart
Is ill adapted to a public part—
Strive to be lenient, not too strictly just,
Praise where you can—blame only where you must.

But hark! methinks I hear some whisp'rer say,
"What have these girls to do with Learning, pray?
"And if we grant them some small share of sense,
"Must they at once lay claim to eloquence?"

In eastern climes, where moslem tyrants reign,
The female world is thought a soulless train—
Mere breathing toys, created but to show'r
Guilty delights upon the passing hour.
No guide for them points out the narrow way
That leads the pure in heart to realms of day:

No kindly spirit turns their gaze on high,
And bids them seek for glories in the sky:
No warning accents reach them from the tomb,
To tell the guilty soul its final doom:
Careless they glide along life's ebbing wave,
Without one wish, one thought beyond the grave,
And quite resign'd, when death shall close the eye,
To sink in silence, and forgotten lie.

But we who live where happier fates controul,
Have amply proved that woman has a soul;
A soul as rich in intellectual stores,
As large, as Godlike, haughty man, as yours;
And many a deed to Fame's loud trump consign'd,
Bears noble witness for the female mind.
'Twere vain for me, in my rude verse to tell
With what high names Fame's dazzling records swell:
Go, read them there, where high they stand sublime,
Beyond the reach of Fate, the grasp of Time!
There Edgeworth's shines, whose pen's persuasive pow'r
Shall lend a charm to many a tedious hour,
Shall many a heart with seraph-strains beguile,
And light the cheek of woe with rapture's smile.
Go learn from her, without the female hand,
To scatter flow'rs along life's barren strand,
To smooth your path as on thro' years you go,
This world would be a sterile world of woe,
With not one charm to sooth or power to bless —
But a wide waste of lonely wretchedness.

Remember too, to woman is consign'd
The arduous task to guide the youthful mind;
To rear those tender plants, which, as they grow,
May prove a nation's weal—or nation's woe.
Who nurs'd the patriot spark that burst so bright,
In vengeful fires, on man's astonish'd sight,
When first arose Columbia's darling son—
The good—the *great*—the matchless *Washington?*

'Twas woman's task—weak woman's—to controul
The latent powers of his mighty soul,
'Twas her's to guide the giant arm that hurl'd
The tyrant's myriads from this western world,

To prompt the voice that from the Spartan's grave,
Call'd weeping Freedom o'er the Atlantic wave;
'Twas hers to lead him to that height of Fame,
Where, in eternal splendour shines his name,
With Glory's brightest, rosiest wreath intwin'd,
The ceaseless theme of plaudits to mankind.

And can you, then, deny to her who cheers
Your tedious journey thro' this vale of tears,
(Like you, the wand'rer of a stormy day,)
The light of knowledge to illume the way?
You smile! ah, then I see we've gain'd our cause
And she who merits, will obtain applause.

Lines on the Mounds of Cahokia *

The sun's last rays were fading from the west,
The deepening shades stole slowly o'er the plain.
The evening breeze had lulled itself to rest;
And all was silent; save the mournful strain,
With which the widowed turtle wooed in vain
Her absent lover to her lonely nest.

Now, one by one, emerging to the sight,
The brighter stars assumed their seats on high.
The moon's pale crescent glowed serenely bright;
As the last twilight fled along the sky.
And all her train, in cloudless majesty
Were glittering on the dark, blue vault of night.

I lingered, by some soft enchantment bound;
And gazed, enraptured, on the lovely scene.
From the dark summit of an Indian mound
I saw the plain, outspread in softened green,
Its fringe of hoary cliffs, by moonlight sheen,
And the dark line of forest, sweeping round.

I saw the lesser mounds, which round me rose.
Each was a giant mass of slumbering clay.
There slept the warriors, women, friends, and foes;
There, side by side, the rival chieftains lay;
And mighty tribes, swept from the face of day,
Forgot their wars, and found a long repose.

Ye mouldering relicks of departed years!
Your names have perished; not a trace remains;
Save, where the grass-grown mound its summit rears,
From the green bosom of your native plains.

* from *The Hunter and Other Poems* (1826). The Indian mounds referred
  to are some miles north of Cahokia and have currently been the subject of
  controversy over a proposed highway route which would cut through them.

Say! do your spirits wear oblivion's chains?
Did Death forever quench your hopes and fears?

Or live they, shrined in some congenial form?
What, if the swan, who leaves her summer nest
Among the northern lakes, and mounts the storm,
To wing her rapid flight to climes more blest
Should hover o'er the very spot, where rest
The crumbling bones, once with her spirit warm.

What, if the song, so soft, so sweet, so clear,
Whose music fell so gently from on high,
In tones aerial, thrilling my rapt ear;
Though not a speck was on the cloudless sky,
Were their own soft, funereal melody,
While lingering o'er the scenes, that once were dear.

Or did those fairy hopes of future bliss,
Which simple nature to your bosoms gave,
Find other worlds, with fairer skies than this,
Beyond the gloomy portals of the grave,
In whose bright bowers the virtuous, and the brave
Rest from their toils, and all their cares dismiss?

Where the great hunter still pursues the chase;
And o'er the sunny mountains tracks the deer;
Or finds again each long extinguished race;
And sees once more the mighty mammoth rear
The giant form, which lies embedded here,
Of other years the sole remaining trace.

Or, it may be, that still ye linger near
The sleeping ashes, once your dearest pride;
And, could your forms to mortal eye appear,
Could the dark veil of death be thrown aside;
Then might I see your restless shadows glide
With watchful care, around these relicks dear.

If so, forgive the rude, unhallowed feet,
Which trode so thoughtless o'er your mighty dead.
I would not thus profane their lone retreat;
Nor trample, where the sleeping warrior's head

Lay pillowed on its everlasting bed,
Age after age, still sunk in slumbers sweet

Farewell; and may you still in peace repose.
Still o'er you may the flowers, untrodden, bloom.
And gently wave to every wind, that blows,
Breathing their fragrance o'er each lonely tomb,
Where, earthward mouldering, in the same dark womb,
Ye mingle with the dust, from whence ye rose.

The Silent Monks *

Amidst the hundred mounds, that rise
Above Cahokia's flowering plains, I spent
A vernal day. The cloudless sun rode high,
And all was silent, save that in the air,
Above the fleecy clouds, careering swans,
With trumpet note, sailed slowly to the south;
And a soft breeze swept gently o'er the grass;
Moving its changing verdure, like the wave.
A few religious mid these sepulchers
Had fixed their home. In sackcloth clad they were;
And they were old and gray, and walked as in dreams,
Emaciate, sallow, pale. Their furrowed brow,
Though now subdued, show'd many a trace
That stormy passions once had wantoned there.
I asked the way, the country, and the tombs.
One finger on their lip, the other hand
Raised to the sky, they motion'd me
That they were vowed to silence, and might give
No ascent to their thoughts, 'Twas said around.
That they had deeply sinn'd beyond the seas.
That one had practiced cruel perjury
To a fond heart, that broke, when he proved false;
And sunk in beauty's blighted bloom to earth.
Another, for an idle fray in wine, that rose
For venal beauty, slew his dearest friend.
A third, like Lucifer, had fall'n from power.
They all had play'd high parts; had been

* from William T. Coggeshall's *The Poets and Poetry of the West* (1860). The reference here is to a short-lived Trappist monastery that was located near the largest of the mounds mentioned in the preceding poem.

Where pageants, music, beauty, wine, and mirth,
Ambition, favor, grandeur, all that glares,
A king and courtiers, hated and caress'd,
In seeming held the keys of love and joy.
Remorse had smitten them. Her snakes had stung
Their hearts; and the deep voice, that all on earth
Is vanity, had scattered their dreams.
They clad themselves in hair, and took a vow
To break their silence only at the tomb.*
Haply, they thought to fly from their dark hearts;
And they came o'er the billow, wand'ring still
Far to the west. Here, midst a boundless waste
Of rank and gaudy flowers, and o'er the bones
Of unknown races of the ages past,
They dwelt. Themselves knew not the deep, dark thoughts
Of their associates. When the unbidden tear
Rose to their eye, they dashed away to earth
The moisture; but might never tell the source
Whence it was sprung; nor joy, nor hope, nor grief,
Nor fear might count, or tell, or share their throbs.
When sweet remembrance of the past came o'er
Their minds in joy, no converse of those years
Might soothe the present sadness of their state.
Man's heart is made of iron, or 'twould burst
'Midst mute endurances of woes, like these.
I saw the sun behind the western woods
Go down upon their shorn and cowled heads.
No vesper hymn consoled their troubled thoughts.
Far o'er the plain the wolf's lugubrious howl,
The crickets chirp, and the nocturnal cry
Of hooting owls, was their sad evening song.

* By their vows they were permitted to speak just before death. [note in
Coggeshall]

The Indian Maid's Death Song *

The valiant Dakota has gone to the chase,
The pride of my heart and the hope of his race;
His arrows are sharp, and his eye is true
And swift is the march of his birchen canoe;
But suns shall vanish, and seasons shall wane,
Ere the hunter shall clasp his WINONA again!

Away, you falsehearted, who smile to destroy,
Whose hearts plan deceit, while your lips utter joy;
Winona is true to the vow she has made,
And none but the hunter shall win the dark maid.
I sing my death dirge for the grave I prepare;
And soon shall my true lover follow me there.

His heart is so true, that in death he shall not
Forget the sad scene of this blood sprinkled spot;
But swift as the foot of the light-bounding doe,
He'll fly through the regions of darkness below,
To join his Winona in mansions of truth,
Where love burns eternal, with beauty and youth.

Stern sire, and false-hearted kingsmen, adieu!
I sing my death song, and my courage is true;
'Tis painful to die—but the pride of my race
Forbids me to pause betwixt pain and disgrace;
The rocks they are sharp, and the precipice high—
See, see! how a maiden can teach ye to die!

* from William T. Coggeshall's *The Poets and Poetry of the West* (1860).

A Sketch *

'Twas summer in the land: thick leaves and flowers,
Tall grass and grain were on the lap of June,
The yellow sunlight trembled on the hills,
The dewy hills fresh with the breath of morn;
And o'er them smiled the golden summer skies,
When with blank book and manual I went
To gather wildflowers in the forest shade;
Wide roving then I found a beauteous spot,
Lonely and lovely, where a rapid stream
Comes from the eastward through a narrow pass,
O'erhung with mossy rocks and bending woods,
Then southward wanders in broad meadow ground.

Stranger! if thou wouldst leave for nature's peace
Earth's eating strifes, come to this lonely spot,
And by the river's angle sit thee down;
Thine eye shall see far east, the narrow bed
Of the dark stream, o'erarched with woven boughs,
Impervious to the sun, and fenced with rocks;
Ragged and high, moist with the trickling drops,
And decked with fern and lichen; while below,
The current steals with gladness o'er its bed
Of smooth worn stones; and toward the noonday sun,
Broad meadows, widening fast as they recede,
Covered with summer bloom, shall meet thine eye;
Crowfoot, geranium, and columbine,
All mingled, and all wavering in the wind,
The soft sweet wind, that comes to fan thy cheek;
And o'er all these, stretched out in loveliness,
The summer heaven, lofty and lighted up
With the great sun, through all its azure depths;
Near thee the silent bird shall leave the bough,
To taste the running stream. And thou shalt look
Upon its glassy breast, and see thy form,

* from the *Illinois Monthly Magazine* (September, 1831).

In due proportions, all reflected fair;
The rippling wave shall pour its quiet voice
Into thy listening ear; earth's mingled charms
Shall touch thy soul with magic, and heaven's peace
Shall fill thy gladdened heart. Thy passions here
Shall bow themselves and die; all, all, save love,
And that shall be alone: even the thought
Of thy existence shall no more be thine,
Till the strong spell that chains thy soul be past.

Hymn *

*Sung at the Congregational Church, at Princeton, at the
last service held in their old house of Worship, 1845.*

Almighty God! for many a year
Have we, Thy children, gathered here;
And now, within this humble house,
Have come to pay our parting vows.

Ah! Wondrous years! within the range
Of human sight, what mighty change!
And backward as we turn our eyes,
What sacred memories arise!

E'er yet these fields by plow were broke,
Or rose in air the village smoke,
Thy servants trenched the virgin sod
And reared this house to Thee, our God.

Here each succeeding Sabbath morn,
'Mid jeers of hate and taunts of scorn,
Few, weak, yet strong in truth, we came
To nurse and spread its kindling flame.

Here has the thoughtless soul been roused,
The sorrowing heart to peace composed;
Here has the cup of joy o'erflowed,
With blessings by Thy hand bestowed.

* This and the poems following are from E. R. Brown's *Life and Poems of
John Howard Bryant* (1894). The dates of the poems range from 1845 to
1871.

Here hath the fleeing bondman found
A shield from Hell's pursuing hound;
And hence have Freedom's truths gone forth
To shake and light and bless the Earth.

With saddened hearts, as duty calls,
We leave these venerated walls,
Nor deem, whate'er may be our lot,
This hallowed place can be forgot.

Hymn *

Upon the nation's heart,
    A mighty burden lies;
Two hundred years of crime and tears,
    Of anguish, groans and sighs.

How long, O Lord! how long!
    Crushed, trampled, peeled and dumb;
Shall thy bound children suffer wrong,
    And no deliverer come?

The eternal years sweep on—
    Age after age, goes by—
Still waits the slave the breaking dawn,
    The day-spring from on high.

"How long, O Lord! how long!"
    When shall that cry to Thee,
Be lost in freedom's glorious song;
    And shouts of jubilee?

A swift, awakening thrill,
    Send through the nation's heart;
Make quick the conscience, pure the will,
    And love of right impart.

Hasten, O Lord, the hour,
    For which we wait and pray;
When Thy resistless breath of power,
    Shall sweep the curse away.

    * written in 1858.

If men refuse, O God,
   To set the captives free;
Break as of old the oppressors' rod,
   And give them liberty.

As Jesus from the tomb,
   The buried Lazarus led;
Rend Thou the slaves' deep night of gloom,
   Oh, raise him from the dead.

Sonnet

I saw a preacher in the house of God,
With frantic gestures and in accents loud,
And words profane he spread his hands abroad
And poured anathemas upon the crowd!
His speech was set with many a phrase uncouth,
And frivolous remark and common jest;
A mixture strange of folly and of truth,
With fierce denunciations for the rest.
Is this, I thought while listening to his strains,
A follower of the meek and lowly one?
Are these the accents heard on Bethlehm's plains,
When angels hailed the birth of Mary's Son?
Is this the Gospel sent us from above
Whose words are peace and charity and love?

Death of Lincoln

"Make way for liberty," cried Winkelried,
   And gathered to his breast the Austrian spears.
Fired with fresh valor at the glorious deed,
   O'er the dead hero rushed those mountaineers
To victory and freedom. Even so
   Our dear, good Lincoln fell in freedom's cause.
And while our hearts are pierced with keenest woe,
   Lo, the black night of slavery withdraws,
And liberty's bright dawn breaks o'er the land.
   Four million bondmen, held in helpless thrall,
Loosed by his word, in nature's manhood stand,
   And the sweet sun of peace shines over all.
The blood that stained the martyr's simple robe
   Woke the deep sympathies of half the globe.

Drought

Not a cloud in the sky, but a brassy haze,
   Through which the sun glares hot and red,
Day after day, these long June days,
   'Till the grass is withered and the flowers are dead.

I sit by my home and gaze away,
   For some sign of rain in the burning sky—
Some mist, or cloud, or vapor gray,
   Till the day fades on my weary eye.

The birds that sang by my door have flown,
   The bluebird, the oriole and wren,
Even the robin that steals my cherries has gone,
   To the cooler shade o'er the brook in the glen.

The maize plant droops in the mid day sun,
   But rallies at eventide again;
Looking up to heaven when day is done,
   And sighs in the wind as if sighing for rain.

From the bosom of earth goes up a sigh,
   From every living thing a plaint;
The leaves on the shrubs are crisp and dry,
   And the mighty woods look sick and faint.

O! for the faith and prayer of Him,
   Who bowed upon Carmel's mount of yore;
When rose on the far horizon's rim,
   The little cloud with its priceless store.

"But those times of undoubting faith are past,"
   Men say, "And the age of law has come,
Trust in the Lord is waning fast,
   And His prophets of power are dead or dumb."

A Winter Morning on the Prairie *

The storm has ceased! All nature hushed and still,
Enshrouded in one sheet of crystal lies.
Now forth walks joyous, with industrious eyes,
The early poet, musing journey's fill.
Yes, this is nature's magic! This the skill
Her hand evinces, through the varied year!
What sweet enchantment reigns in every scene!
In spring, from earth's uprising, all is green;
In summer, fields of white and gold appear;
In autumn, party-colored woods are sere;
In each stream's murmur, zephyrs, softly bland,
Wave o'er the lawn, and sway the forest tops,
Birds choir, flowers breathe, or withered verdure drops.
Now, stark, and motionless, each twig must stand,
Streams bound, birds mute, flowers dead;
    fast by her potent wand.

And thus the bard, in audible delight.
Deep blazing monarch, ushered by the morn,
Glances with majesty, wide o'er the lawn,
And all, erst swaddled in transparent white,
With dazzling lustre overcomes the sight,
The spriggy tree tops, fiercely sparkling, seem
Vast branching pearls, with glittering pendants hung,
The scattered cottages, with many a gleam,
For flashing, broad effulgence stream;
Heaped cones of plenty all ablaze are seen,
Bright zig zag fences teem with shreds of glass,
The bristled stubble fields a glowing mass;
Each upright blade a staff, and the whole scene,
Groves, farm yards, streams, and plain, one
    glaring waste of sheen.

* This and the two poems following are from *Miscellaneous Poems* (1845).

About Our Late Indian Hunt

Say! Did you hear of Black Hawk's war,
Where nature's own was struggled for?
Terror struck all the country through,
Raised by aggressors bugaboo!
   A few poor Indians cornered up,
Saw, day by day, the Whites usurp
Their last game grounds, their childhood homes,
And even profane their father's tombs.
They saw, they wept with deep still grief;
Hope held no prospect of relief;
"Farther, yet farther we must go:
Swim to new wilds, like buffalo!"
They bore in silence, 'till their wives,
"Whipped like the dogs, we loathe our lives"
'Till from their mouths was snatched their bread;
'Till the last star of peace had sped.
Then roused they pride's expiring ray,
Their thickening deaths to hold at bay:
They roused for home, they stood for life;
Peace heaped them wrongs; wrongs called for strife.
Blow came for blow; the cry was raised,
"Behold the savage fury blazed,
The frontier wide in ruin lies!"
"Death to the race! – the aggressor cries –
Death to the race! Yes, when no more
They turned the cheek, as heretofore,
'Tis "savage fury" prompts the stand,
On the last hold of childhood's land!
   Take back the term! The wildman's heart
Abhors the deeds of savage art!
Expiring, starved, they fled like dear;
Still, still the gorgeless hounds pressed near.
   Wiskenan, and the Broad-Axe tell
Tales which your final dirge may knell!
A war! Alas! a ruthless chase,
For famished remnants of a murdered race.

A Prairie Song

O! Some may choose the forest glade,
    And some may love the sea,
Others may seek the city's din,
    But none of these for me.

No hermit's cave, no crowded hive,
    No storm-tossed prison lone;
For life at ease, in joys own breeze,
    A prairie cot my own.

A prairie cot! What joys do not
    Come clustering round the charm;
Scarce ripening fruits to Autumn cling,
    As pleasures hither swarm!

Dream, hunters, dream, of seas of game,
    Unused to following hound;
The generous Lord, his bounteous board,
    And plenty laughing round.

Dream of the lass, who makes her glass,
    Her conscious lover's heart;
Who, decked with smiles, knows ought of wiles,
    And plays well nature's part.

Dream of the home, where hearts have room,
    Where nice restraint is not;
Dream, dream, of joy free from alloy,
    Found in the Prairie Cot.

O! Some may choose the forest glade,
    And some may love the sea,
While others, seek the city's din
    The prairie life give me.

Here, Clara, here, love's mutual care
    Shall smile around our hearth,
While, hand in hand, we prove the land
    The Paradise of Earth.

Farewell to Illinois *

Illinois, adieu to thy flies and mosquitoes,
　　Thy black, muddy roads, with their soil three feet deep;
I was anxious to gaze on thy beautiful features,
　　But in parting I feel no desire to weep.

Farewell to thy dark green alluvial ocean,
　　Thy rank waving tall grass and cattle in herds;
Thy "fever and ague," creating emotion
　　Expressive of feelings much louder than words.

I passed o'er thy valley by day and nocturnal,
　　Thy sun made my head ache, thy moon gave a chill;
And I now write it down for my friends and the Journal,
　　'Tis my first and last visit, let what happen will.

I had heard of thy beauty, been told of thy treasures,
　　Of thy wild game and wild flowers "blushing unseen";
I long had been anxious to taste of thy pleasures,
　　Forgetting that pleasures were followed by pain.

Adieu, Illinois! and to all thy pale livers,
　　Thy lily-faced ladies and yellow-skinned men,
I entered thee smiling, and leave with the shivers;
　　Let other folks love thee, but I never can.

* Published in the Newton *Journal* (1847). Given here as printed in the *Journal of the Illinois Historical Society,* Vol. 14 (April–January, 1921–22), 334–35.

Illinois *

A country in the distant west
With fertile soil is largely blest
With prairies spreading wide;
In summer time full dress'd in green
Like meadows large, they may be seen
With blossoms deck'd in pride.

Here Nature's gifts are lavished wide
Profusely as an eastern bride
With gems be-spangled o'er;
And when the sun to rest retires
And smothers out his radiant fires,
By us is seen no more.

In slumbers sweet he dreams all night
Of beauteous scenes that caught his sight
This country trav'ling o'er;
And when he wakes at break of day
On golden cars he rides away
To view this land once more.

He calls up then the moon his bride
And down he sits near by her side
And takes her by the hand;
If ever I shall cease to run
And be to earth a radiant sun
I'll settle in this land.

* This and the poems following are from *Poems for the Old and the Young* (1857).

The Evils of Slavery

The curse of Slavery, I sing,
To view its hideous picture bring,
Nor let the glimpse offend the sight
Although as dark as lonely night.
Nor let the South who own the slaves
Suppose I take them all for knaves —
As noble hearts in Southern lands
Beat, as the wide, wide world commands.
The Southern climes so balmy are
The winds so soft, the skies so clear,
That hospitality's sweet reign
Comes walking in the pleasing train.
Then why the Southern customs blame
For were we there we'd be the same,
All Southern men the evil see
And know its wrongs as well as we.
But evils that we cannot cure
With fortitude we must endure,
And if we mind our own affairs
May rest assur'd the South will theirs.
Come let us now the states compare
Where slavery is and taints the air,
With those that ever have been free
As winds that blow from sea to sea.
And for example let us take
Kentucky as a slavery state,
And it with Illinois compare
Where freedom breaths its native air.
So wide the difference seems to be
It must be caus'd by slavery,
Now let us travel farther west
Select Missouri as a test,
To all its worth give justice sway
And by her side set Iowa.
Missouris worth her charms are gone
And Iowa bears the triumph home,
So the fair Moon withdraws her light
When golden Sol appears in sight.
And while the passing muse now sings
The woful sights that slavery brings,
I see the lash and hear the sound

That makes the body all one wound.
My soul the sight abhors to see
Disgusted turns from misery,
But what, shall Northern men now say
That we will steal the Slaves away?
This only makes the matter worse,
As one that loses his best horse
More closely watches for the thief
And hears the rustling of the leaf,
That hangs upon the distant trees
And quivers to the midnight breeze.
Then if the thing I rightly scan,
It surely is the wisest plan,
To mind at home our own affairs,
Let Southern men attend to theirs.

Address to the Father of Waters

Majestic stream that sweetly glides
Through fertile valleys, long and wide,
Where Red Men once did roam;
What power Divine first bade thee flow,
And scoop'd thy channel wide and low
Through beds of gravelly stone?

"The same kind hand who form'd the skies,
And dipp'd the rainbows in the dies
Of variagated hue,
Spake and I heard the God-like sound,
My way through shelving rocks I wound,
And paid my homage due."

Then speed thee in thy course sublime,
Nor stop to ask of fate the time
That winding thou must roll,
But onward rush with mighty force,
'Till God shall hail thee in thy course
And shake the distant Pole.

Then cease to flow, O stream sublime,
For then shall come the end of Time,
And Nature vast shall die,
Nor naught shall then remain of thee,
Nor yet of earth or peaceful sea
Or stars above the sky.

Noble Illinois *

"It is men that make the State."
SCHUYLER COLFAX

Fetch me the maps, gazetteers and old chronicles,
    Gather the records of ages long told;
Count me the deeds of the brave knights of chivalry,
    Bring out fair laurel-wreaths centuries old;
        Sing me the sweetest songs
        Uttered by minstrel tongues,
Read me the proudest old epic e'er penned;
        Whisper the fairy tales
        Gleaned from sequestered vales,
Name me the friend that proved truest to friend!

Out on those maps trace each grand principality,
    Kingdoms and empires — a famous array!
Yet I'll discover to thousands of loyal hearts
    One bright spot dearer and fairer than they.
        Beautiful, stalwart State —
        Illinois, strong and great!
Thine be the name whose glad praises we sound;
        Annals of thee shall dim
        All those old records grim;
Further, the deeds of thy heroes resound!

Still more enduring the leaves of the laurel-wreath
    Twined o'er the brows of thine honored ones seem;
Here, in thy vigor, thy freshness and purity,
    Brighter the dreams which thy poets shall dream.
        Here shall the minstrel breeze
        Play, o'er the flowery leas,
Music far sweeter than lute ever gave;
        Or, by the low heaped mound,
        There it shall sadly sound
Requiems over the patriot's grave!

* from the *Western Monthly* (Chicago, May, 1869).

Beautiful Prairie-land, flecked with white cottages,
    Like the fair lilybells nestled in green,
Nor for the fullness of nature's rich treasured stores
    Honor ye have among nations, I ween.
        Not for your plains alone,
        Not for the wealth ye own,
But for your true-hearted children of worth;
        Noble of heart and great
        Men it is make the State,
Giving thee beautiful fame in the earth!

The Wedded Waters *

Far from life's busy scenes and bustling crowds,
  Where snow-crowned mountains fondly kiss the clouds,
Missouri, daughter of the glorious West,
                    Sprang into light.

Pure infant streamlet, like a silver thread
Unwinding seaward, as by fancy led,
Thou fall'st from craggy rocks in bright cascades
                    And crystal rills.

Earth's garnered treasures yield a gleam of ore,
A touch of beauty from her precious store;
From hidden cleft thou comest murmuring forth
                    O'er sands of gold.

The gathered waters from unnumbered streams,
Brewed 'mid the rocks, distilled in deep ravines,
Unite with babbling brooks from gushing springs,
                    To swell thy form.

Streamlet no longer, but a river grand —
Broad, rushing, regal, proudest in the land —
Sweep onward; in thy mighty majesty
                    Thou reign'st a queen.

From distant clime, where pure Itasca glows,
Great Mississippi, fed by northern snows,
With waves murm'ring sweet music, southward sped
                    To claim his bride.

Ere yet the Indian, in his birch canoe,
With arrowy speed adown the waters flew,
In fond embrace the beauteous rivers met,
                    Never to part.

* from the *Western Monthly* (Chicago, April, 1869).

Sun, moon and stars joined in the marriage chimes;
All nature's voices woke in heavenly rhymes;
No human presence marred the glorious scene
Of perfect joy.

Lo! in a mighty and harmonious one,
The wedded waters sweep beneath the sun,
Brightening the shores while journeying oceanward
With ceaseless flow.

Whether in ice-locked fetters winter-bound,
Or softly flowing with melodious sound,
Flashing in sunshine, whitening in the storm,
United still.

Symbol most perfect of a marriage true,
By hosts *attempted,* but *attained* by few;
Union sublime—two blended into one—
Forevermore!

Benedicite *

In all the hours thy future may command,
May the rich blessings of the Father's hand
Make glad the way before thy coming feet.
Behold, where thou must go I hear the sweet
Far voice of Spring eternal. On thy way
There falls the radiance of undying day.
No more thy heart o'er vanished treasure grieves,
Borne on the blast like autumn's scarlet leaves;
For on the fire-swept plain, in gleaming lines
The magic of thy New Creation shines.
O risen one! a glory doth enfold
Thy sack-cloth robe transmuted into gold!
O City, purged by sacramental flame,
Be great in virtue, as thou art in name!
Within thy walls may Happiness abide;
Mercy and Peace dwell ever side by side;
May Plenty smile; and Concord be confessed,
With sweet Content, in every home a guest.
And far away without thine open gate
Be Rapine, Discord, Avarice, and Hate.
God grant to thee and thine a noble fame,
And guard thee well from pestilence and flame,
From dire oppression and the bloody sword; —
And may the blessing of the gracious Lord,
Which maketh rich and adds no sorrow then,
Abide in peace with thee and thine. Amen

* from the *Lakeside Monthly* (Chicago, October, 1873—special number on the "recompletion of the city" following the 1871 fire).

The Prairie *

The skies are blue above my head,
    The prairie green below,
And flickering o'er the tufted grass
    The shifting shadows go,
Vague-sailing, where the feathery clouds
    Fleck white the tranquil skies,
Black javelins darting where aloft
    The whirring pheasant flies.

A glimmering plain in drowsy trance
    The dim horizon bounds,
Where all the air is resonant
    With sleepy summer sounds, —
The life that sings among the flowers,
    The lisping of the breeze,
The hot cicala's sultry cry,
    The murmurous dream of bees.

The butterfly — a flying flower —
    Wheels swift in flashing rings,
And flutters round his quiet kin,
    With brave flame-mottled wings.
The wild Pinks burst in crimson fire,
    The Phlox' bright clusters shine,
And Prairie-Cups are swinging free
    To spill their airy wine.

And lavishly beneath the sun,
    In liberal splendor rolled,
The Fennel fills the dipping plain
    With floods of flowery gold;

---

* This and the poems following are from *The Complete Poetical Works of John Hay* (1913). The date of "The Prairie" is 1858. "Jim Bludso" and "Banty Tim" are from *Pike County Ballads*, 1871.

And widely weaves the Iron-Weed
    A woof of purple dyes
Where Autumn's royal feet may tread
    When brankrupt Summer flies.

In verdurous tumult far away
    The prairie-billows gleam,
Upon their crests in blessing rests
    The noontide's gracious beam.
Low quivering vapors steaming dim
    The level splendors break
Where languid Lilies deck the rim
    Of some land-circled lake.

Far in the East like low-hung clouds
    The waving woodlands lie;
Far in the West the glowing plain
    Melts warmly in the sky.
No accent wounds the reverent air,
    No footprint dints the sod, —
Lone in the light the prairie lies,
    Rapt in a dream of God.

Jim Bludso
Of the Prairie Belle

Wall, no! I can't tell you whar he lives,
    Becase he don't live, you see;
Leastways, he's got out of the habit
    Of livin' like you and me.
Whar have you been for the last three year
    That you haven't heard folks tell
How Jimmy Bludso passed in his checks
    The night of the Prairie Belle?

He weren't no saint, — them engineers
    Is all pretty much alike, —
One wife in Natchez-under-the-Hill
    And another one here, in Pike;
A keerless man in his talk was Jim,
    And an awkward hand in a row,

But he never flunked, and he never lied, —
    I reckon he never knowed how.

And this was all the religion he had, —
    To treat his engine well;
Never be passed on the river;
    To mind the pilot's bell;
And if ever the Prairie Belle took fire, —
    A thousand times he swore,
He'd hold her nozzle agin the bank
    Till the last soul got ashore.

All boats has their day on the Mississip,
    And her day come at last, —
The Movastar was a better boat,
    But the Belle she *wouldn't* be passed.
And so she come tearin' along that night —
    The oldest craft on the line —
With a nigger squat on her safety-valve,
    And her furnace crammed, rosin and pine.

The fire bust out as she clared the bar,
    And burnt a hole in the night,
And quick as a flash she turned, and made
    For that willer-bank on the right.
There was runnin' and cursin', but Jim yelled out,
    Over all the infernal roar,
"I'll hold her nozzle agin the bank
    Till the last galoot's ashore."

Through the hot, black breath of the burnin' boat
    Jim Bludso's voice was heard,
And they all had trust in his cussedness,
    And knowed he would keep his word.
And, sure's you're born, they all got off
    Afore the smokestacks fell, —
And Bludso's ghost went up alone
    In the smoke of the Prairie Belle.

He wern't no saint, — but at jedgment
    I'd run my chance with Jim,
'Longside of some pious gentlemen
    That wouldn't shook hands with him.

He seen his duty, a dead-sure thing, —
    And went for it thar and then;
And Christ ain't a-going to be too hard
    On a man that died for men.

Banty Tim

    (Remarks of Sergeant Tilmon Joy to the White Man's Com-
      mittee of Spunky Point, Illinois)

I reckon I git your drift, gents, —
    You 'low the boy sha'n't stay;
This is a white man's country;
    You're Dimocrats, you say;
And whereas, and seein', and wherefore,
    The times bein' all out o' j'int,
The nigger has got to mosey
    From the limits o' Spunky P'int!

Le's reason the thing a minute:
    I'm an old-fashioned Dimocrat too,
Though I laid my politics out o' the way
    For to keep till the war was through.
But I come back here, allowin'
    To vote as I used to do,
Though it gravels me like the devil to train
    Along o' sich fools as you.

Now dog my cats ef I kin see,
    In all the light of the day,
What you've got to do with the question
    Ef Tim shill go or stay.
And furder than that I give notice,
    Ef one of you tetches the boy,
He kin check his trunks to a warmer clime
    Than he'll find in Illanoy.

Why, blame your hearts, jest hear me!
    You know that ungodly day
When our left struck Vicksburg Heights, how ripped
    And torn and tattered we lay.

When the rest retreated I stayed behind,
    Fur reasons sufficient to me, —
With a rib caved in, and a leg on a strike,
    I sprawled on that cursed glacee.

Lord! how the hot sun went for us,
    And br'iled and blistered and burned!
How the Rebel bullets whizzed round us
    When a cuss in his death-grip turned!
Till along toward dusk I seen a thing
    I couldn't believe for a spell:
That nigger—that Tim—was a-crawlin' to me
    Through that fire-proof, gilt-edged hell!

The Rebels seen him as quick as me,
    And the bullets buzzed like bees;
But he jumped for me, and shouldered me,
    Though a shot brought him once to his knees;
But he staggered up, and packed me off,
    With a dozen stumbles and falls,
Till safe in our lines he drapped us both,
    His black hide riddled with balls.

So, my gentle gazelles, thar's my answer,
    And here stays Banty Tim:
He trumped Death's ace for me that day,
    And I'm not goin' back on him!
You may rezoloot till the cows come home,
    But ef one of you tetches the boy.
He'll wrastle his hash to-night in hell,
    Or my name's not Tilmon Joy.

2. TURNINGS

CONCERNED as it is with the poets who wrote chiefly in the late years of the nineteenth century and the very early years of the twentieth, Part II marks, at the very least, a turning chronologically. But more is involved, for while a number of the selections indicate a continuation of the verse characteristics observed in "Some Beginnings," there is a discernible shift qualitatively. Taking the poetry of this period in its entirety, the earlier genteel and even amateurish characteristics, occasionally still evident, are being displaced by elements quite different. In part these "turnings" can be noticed in subject matter—for example, the increase in urban topics—but more importantly in a sharper critical spirit, a greater and yet freer sense of form, and a developing poetic taste. Certainly the work of such a poet as William Vaughn Moody displays an indisputable growth in poetic maturity, and he is not alone. The choice of poems for this part of the anthology has been made with a view to exemplifying these shifts in the character of poetry in Illinois, as in American poetry more broadly viewed; but there has also been a continued effort to select poems with Illinois sectional qualities, including the less obvious midwest sensibilities and social attitudes. The 1915 date as a terminus is, of course, somewhat arbitrarily chosen and might well have been set some years either way; moreover, several poets whose work extends into later years, might have been included in the next section—though with rare exceptions the particular poems presented were written within the 1880–1915 period.

Ernest McGaffey, whose poetry opens this division, was professionally a lawyer in Chicago and for some years literary critic of the Chicago *American*. His work reveals some of the earlier characteristics already noted. These qualities, including a certain sentimentality, are also to be discovered in the poems of Horace Fiske, though there is in his work a much stronger flavor of the urban. Through the years of his writing extending well into the twentieth century, Fiske was connected with the University of Chicago in various positions ranging from that of lecturer on English literature to that of University Recorder. Eugene Field, just before the start of the new century, and Bert Leston Taylor, just after, as newspaper columnists (in the Chicago *Daily News* and the Chicago *Daily Tribune,* respectively) are representative of a journalistic writing that contributed substantially to a more realistic literature in the United States. In their newspaper verse—the humorous and satirical rather than the sentimental—they no doubt played a part in bringing in the sharper poetry of the coming years. Harriet Monroe of Chicago, later instrumental through her editorship of *Poetry, A Magazine of Verse* in stimulating the New Poetry, wrote poetry of a kind and chiefly at a time that places her in the present period rather than the next. William Vaughn Moody is biographically connected with Illinois through his teaching at the University of Chicago in the closing years of the nineteenth century. A more significant linkage, however, is revealed in the liberal critical attitudes of much of his poetry, probably derived in part from his midwest background, but certainly much more from his University associations. Edith Wyatt and Florence Kiper Frank, again both Chicago-based poets, perhaps stand closest to the New Poetry, and the inclusion of samples of their poetry helps to make evident the "turnings" of Part II.

The Meadow-Lark *

A sea of grass on either side
The prairie stretches far and wide,
Its undulating line of blades
Reflects the noontide lights and shades,
And brings before me one by one
The pictures wrought by wind and sun.

And silence reigns, save for the breeze
And muffled hum of droning bees,
Till in the summer hush I hear
A prairie signal sweet and clear,
In mournful, piercing notes that mark
The whistle of the meadow-lark.

Like one wild cry for loved and lost
From some lone spirit tempest-tossed,
It wails across the waving grass,
And, blending with the winds that pass,
It scatters echoes at my feet
So full of pain, so deadly sweet.

Oh! heart of hearts, could my unrest
Find such a song within my breast,
My passionate and yearning cry
Would echo on from sea to sky,
Along the path of future years,
And touch the listening world to tears.

* This and the following poem, "The Message of the Town," are from *Poems* (1895).

The Message of the Town

Look up to the stony arches
Where art and mammon meet,
There's a sound where Traffic marches
A call in the City street,
    For a voice is ever ringing
    "Gird up your loins and flee
    I will harden your heart or break it
    If you will abide with me."

Go forth with a noble yearning,
Give heed to the griefs of men,
And the years will find you turning
To that mocking voice again,
    Which ever recurrent whispers
    Like the chant of the restless sea
    "I will harden your heart or break it
    If you will abide with me."

No time for the touch of gladness
Nor yet for the boon of tears,
We toss in a cloud of madness
Whirled round by the whirling years,
    And an echo lingers always
    From which we are never free
    "I will harden your heart or break it
    If you will abide with me."

Aye! carve it in iron letters
High over your widest gate,
Since we all must wear the fetters
Who seek the appointed fate,
    And the winds shall bring the message
    Through all of the days that be
    "I will harden your heart or break it
    If you will abide with me."

From a City Roof *
South Park, Chicago

On the deck of my big night steamer, aloft in my low sea-chair,
Wrapped round with a southern softness and breathing a sweet sea
air,
I sail of a summer evening beneath a starry sky,
And wonder long at the beauty that never passes by.

For I see on the far-off Temple a crown of softened light
That rests like a golden glory on the city in its might;
And off at the harbor's entrance, where the piers push long and dark,
The red and yellow beacon flashes out its shining mark.

And down past the lone Rabida, below the reddened cloud,
Flame up the leaping torches where the ranks of labor crowd;
Till my eye goes wandering lakeward where the constellations move
Of the hidden ships that pass and their pilot's eye approve.

The Midway's glittering pageant, reaching down from park to park,
Shoots a thousand cycle-signals through the scintillating dark;
And the studious windows shining in the Varsity's looming walls
Mark off in mellow outline the gray old Gothic halls.

And all below me gleam the lights of a myriad city homes
That are dearer to the city man than a myriad glittering domes;
For the faces there are glowing with a love that keeps him strong
And comes to his wearied heart and brain like the sweetness of a
song.

So, when the night comes down above the city streets,
And silent-shining star his silent brother greets,
On the deck of my lofty roof I love to take my sail,
And watch the passing lights and the stars that never fail.

* This and the poems following are from *The Ballad of Manilla Bay and Other
Verses* (1900).

Chicago

Erect, commanding, like a goddess born,
    With strength and beauty glowing in her face
    And all her stately form attired in grace,
She stands beside her lake to greet the morn.
Behind her, rustling leaves of yellow corn
    That whisper richest comfort to the race;
    And 'neath her gaze, the waters' purple space
A thousand flashing sails with light adorn.
Still in her sight shine visions of the fair —
    Immortal Art illuming human ill,
And far-eyed Science blessing with her care;
    While through her soul, in purpose to fulfil,
And reach her highest hope beyond compare,
    Throbs deep and strong the strenuous cry: "I will."

The Genius of Hull House

Halsted Street, Chicago

Girt round with misery careless of the light, —
    A motley mass still needing to be one
    In civic hope and happier life begun, —
Her guiding spirit draws from out the night,
She knows the worth of comfort and delight
    To win the soul to sit beneath the sun
    And strive for things that only should be won, —
Forever leading with a clearer sight.
For always to her aid she calls sweet art
    That loves the temple of the human soul,
    To free the mind and bless the wearied heart;
And by a human hand-touch her control
    Becomes of e'en the humblest life a part,
And helps through one the purpose of the whole.

The Liberator
St. Gaudens' Lincoln, Lincoln Park, Chicago

Uprisen from his fascèd chair of state,
    Above his riven people bending grave, —
    His heart upon the sorrow of the slave, —
Stands simply strong the kindly man of fate.
By war's deep bitterness and brothers' hate
    Untouched he stands, intent alone to save
    What God himself and human justice gave, —
The right of men to freedom's fair estate.
In homely strength he towers almost divine,
    His mighty shoulders bent with breaking care,
His thought-worn face with sympathies grown fine;
    And as men gaze, their hearts as oft declare
That this is he whom all their hearts enshrine, —
    This man that saved a race from slow despair.

Human Nature *

A beggar-man crept to my side
    One bitter, wintry time;
"I want to buy a drink," he cried;
    "Please give me, sir, a dime."
If he had craved this boon forlorn
    To buy his family meat,
I had passed on in silent scorn,
    And left him in the street.

I tossed the money in his hand,
    And quoth "As o'er your wine
Within the tippling-room you stand
    Drink thou to me and mine."
He let an earnest "Thank ye" drop—
    Then up the street he sped,
And rushed into a baker's shop,
    And bought a loaf of bread!

I know not why it was, and yet,
    So sudden was the blow,
I felt emotions of regret
    That he had duped me so.
Yet, had the hungry beggar said
    That he was sore in need
Of that necessity called "bread,"
    What man would pay him heed?

* This and the following selections are from *The Poems of Eugene Field* (1949) and appeared originally in his Chicago *Daily News* column "Sharps and Flats," this poem on October 10, 1883.

A Patriot's Triumph *

George William Curtis met a lad
   As down the street he hied.
"Pray tell me, boy, if eke you can,
   Where Schurz † doth now reside."
"In sooth I can, my gentle sir,"
   The honest lad replied;
"Proceed due north and soon you'll come
   To where he doth abide."

"You speak some words I ken not of,"
   George William Curtis cried;
"Now tell in speech non-sectional
   Where doth my friend reside.
I know not north—Schurz knows no south;
   Such terms do ill betide.
The north is south—the south is north—
   The west the east, beside."

"Good sir, you jest," complained the youth,
   And hung his fuddled head.
"Nay, foolish boy, I speak the truth,"
   George William Curtis said;
"Lo, from the south the north wind blows
   And eke the rising tide,
That splashes on our eastern shores,
   Laves all the western side.

"The snows do fall on southern soil
   And on the prairies wide;
The cotton on the northern hills
   Is now the Yankee's pride.
There is no north—there is no south—
   These terms have long since died;

---

* in "Sharps and Flats," November 7, 1883.
† Presumably Carl Schurz (1829–1906), antislavery leader, writer, and civil reformer who came to the United States from Germany in 1852. Curtis (1824–92), of New England, was a writer, editor, and lyceum lecturer, active in the antislavery cause and other reform movements. The poem apparently involves a parodying of Wordsworth's "Resolution and Independence," perhaps by way of Lewis Carroll.

So tell in reconstructed speech
    Where now doth Schurz reside."

"Good master, turn ye to the west,
    And on the eastern side
Adown the northern path, due south,
    Two blocks he doth abide."
George William Curtis missed his way,
    But still it gave him joy
To know our land had gained that day
    A reconstructed boy.

Chicago Weather *

To-day, fair Thisbe, winsome girl!
    Strays o'er the meads where daisies blow,
Or, ling'ring where the brooklets purl,
    Laves in the cool, refreshing flow.

To-morrow, Thisbe, with a host
    Of amorous suitors in her train,
Comes like a goddess forth to coast
    Or skate upon the frozen main.

To-day, sweet posies mark her track,
    While birds sing gayly in the trees;
To-morrow morn, her sealskin sack
    Defies the piping polar breeze.

So Doris is to-day enthused
    By Thisbe's soft, responsive sighs,
And on the morrow is confused
    By Thisbe's cold, repellent eyes.

  * in "Sharps and Flats," December 6, 1884.

When Stedman Comes To Town *

We're cleaning up the boulevards
    And divers thoroughfares;
Our lawns, our fences, and our yards
    Are bristling with repairs;
And soon Chicago 'll be abloom
    With splendor and renown;
For ain't we going to have a boom
    When Stedman comes to town?

And gosh! the things we'll have to eat—
    The things we'll have to drink!
O'er hecatombs of corn-fed meat
    How shall the glasses clink!
Our culture, having started in,
    Will do the thing up brown.
'T will be a race 'twixt brass and tin
    When Stedman comes to town!

There's Mr. Wayback Canvass Hamm,
    Old Croesus' counterpart;
He don't know nor give a damn
    About poetic art;
And he has such amount of pelf
    As would weigh mountains down,
And he has sworn to spread himself
    When Stedman comes to town.

And Mrs. Hamm, a faded belle,
    And one no longer young,—
She speaks the native quite as well
    As any foreign tongue,—
At Mr. Hamm's reception she
    Will wear a gorgeous gown
That shows all else but modesty,
    When Stedman comes to town.

Now, Stedman knows a thing or two
    Besides poetic art;

* in "Sharps and Flats," April 23, 1891. Stedman is E. C. Stedman (1833–1908), poet, critic, editor.

Yes, truth to say, 'twixt me and you,
    Stedmen is mighty smart;
And so I wonder will he smile
    Good-naturedly or frown
At our flamboyant Western style,
    When Stedman comes to town.

Extinct Monsters *

Oh, had I lived in the good old days,
    When the Ichthyosaurus ramped around,
When the Elasmosaur swam the bays,
    And the Sivatherium pawed the ground,
Would I have spent my precious time
At weaving golden thoughts in rhyme?

When the Tinoceras snooped about,
    And the Pterodactyl flapped its wings,
When the Brontops with the warty snout
    Noseyed around for herbs and things,
Would I have bothered myself o'ermuch
About divine afflatus and such?

The Dinotherium flourished then;
    The Pterygotus lashed the seas;
The Rhamphorhynchus prospered when
    The Scaphognathus perched in trees;
And every creature, wild and tame,
Rejoiced in some rococo name.

Pause and ponder; who could write
    A triolet or roundelay
While a Megatherium yawped all night
    And a Hesperornis yamped all day,
While now and again the bray sonorous
Of Glyptodon Asper swelled the chorus?

If I'd been almost anything
    But a poet, I might have got along:
Those extinct monsters of hoof and wing
    Were not conducive to lyric song;
So Nature reserved this tender bard
For the kindlier Age of Pork and Lard.

  * in "Sharps and Flats," May 11, 1893.

The Rime of the Clark Street Cable *
(*Now happily extinct.*)

Twas in a vault beneath the street,
    In the trench of the traction rope,
That I found a guy with a fishy eye
    And a think tank filled with dope.

His hair was matted, his face was black,
    And matted and black was he;
And I heard this wight in the vault recite,
    "In a singular minor key":

"Oh, I am the guy with the fishy eye
    And the think tank filled with dope.
My work is to watch the beautiful botch
    That's known as the Clark Street Rope.

'I pipes my eye as the rope goes by
    For every danger spot.
If I spies one out I gives a shout,
    And we puts in another knot.

'Them knots is all like brothers to me,
    And I loves 'em, one and all."
The muddy guy with the fishy eye
    A muddy tear let fall.

'There goes a knot we tied last week,
    There's one what we tied to-day;
And there's a patch was hard to reach,
    And caused six hours' delay.

---

* "The Rime" and the following verse are from *A Line-O'-Verse or Two* (1911), which, in turn, is a selection from Taylor's Chicago *Daily Tribune* column "A Line-O'-Type or Two" signed "B. L. T." The present "verses" were written in the years from 1909 to 1911.

"Two hundred seventy-nine, all told,
     And I knows their history;
And I'm most attached to a break we patched
     In the winter of 'eighty-three.

"For every time that knot comes round
     It sings out, 'Howdy, Bill!
We'll walk 'em home to-night, old man,
     From here to the Ferris Wheel.

" 'We'll walk 'em in the rush hours, Bill,
     A swearing company,
As we've walked 'em, Bill, since I was tied,
     In the winter of 'eighty-three.' "

The muddy guy with the fishy eye
     Let fall another tear.
"Them knots is wife and child to me;
     I've known 'em forty year.

"For I am the guy with the fishy eye
     And the think tank filled with dope,
Whose work is to watch the lovely botch
     That's known as the Clark Street Rope."

Miss Legion

She is hotfoot after Cultyure,
     She pursues it with a club.
She breathes a heavy atmosphere
Of literary flub.
No literary shrine so far
But she is there to kneel;
          But—
Her favorite line of reading
Is O. Meredith's "Lucille."

Of course she's up on pictures—
Passes for a connoisseur.
On free days at the Institute
You'll always notice her.
She qualifies approval

Of a Titian or Corot;
　　But—
She throws a fit of rapture
When she comes to Bouguereau.

And when you talk of music,
She is Music's devotee.
She will tell you that Beethoven
Always makes her wish to pray;
And "dear old Bach!" His very name
She says, her ear enchants;
　　But—
Her favorite piece is Weber's
"Invitation to the Dance."

Reform in Our Town

There was a man in Our Town
　　And Jimson was his name,
Who cried, "Our civic government
　　Is honeycombed with shame."
He called us neighbors in and said,
　　"By Graft we're overrun.
Let's have a general cleaning up,
　　As other towns have done."

The citizens of Our Town
　　Responded to the call;
Beneath the banner of Reform
　　We gathered one and all
We sent away for men expert
　　In hunting civic sin,
To ask these practised gentlemen
　　Just how we should begin.

The experts came to Our Town
　　And told us how 'twas done.
"Begin with Gas and Traction,
　　And half your fight is won.
Begin with Gas and Traction;
　　The rest will follow soon."

We looked at one another
    And hummed a different tune.

Said Smith, "Saloons in Our Town
    Are palaces of shame."
Said Jones, "Police corruption
    Has hurt the town's fair name."
Said Brown, "Our lawless children
    Pitch pennies as they please."
Now would it not be wiser
    To start Reform with these?

The men who came to Our Town
    Replied, "No haste with these;
Begin with Gas—or Water—
    The roots of the disease."
We looked at one another
    And hemmed and hawed a bit;
Enthusiasm faded then
    From every single cit.

The men who came to Our Town
    Expressed a mild surprise,
Then they too at each other
    Looked "with a wild surmise."
Jimson had stock in Traction,
    And Jones had stock in Gas,
And Smith and Brown in this and that,
    So—nothing came to pass.

The profligates of Our Town
    Pitch pennies as of yore;
Police corruption flourishes
    As rankly as before,
Still are our gilded ginmills
    Foul palaces of shame.
Reform is just as distant
    As when the wise men came.

from the "Columbian Ode" *

O strange divine surprise!
Out of the dark man strives to rise,
And struggles inch by inch with toil and tears;
Till suddenly God stoops from his bright spheres,
    And bares the glory of his face.
    Then darkness flees afar,
    This earth becomes a star—
    Man leaps up to the lofty place.
So these who dared to pass beyond the pale,
For a rash dream tempting the shrouded seas,
Sought but Cathay; God bade their faith prevail
To find a world—blessed his purposes!
The hero knew not what a virgin soul
Laughed through glad eyes when at her feet he laid
The gaudy trappings of man's masquerade.
She who had dwelt in forests, heard the roll
Of lakes down-thundering to the sea,
Beheld from gleaming mountain-heights
Two oceans playing with the lights
Of night and morn—ah! what would she
With all the out-worn pageantry
Of purple robes and heavy mace and crown?
    Smiling she casts them down,
    Unfit her young austerity
Of hair unbound and strong limbs bare and brown.

    Yet they who dare arise
    And meet her stainless eyes
Forget old loves, though crowned queens these be.
    And whither her winged feet fare
    They follow though death be there—

* written for and delivered at the dedication (Columbus Day, 1892) of the
Chicago Exposition of 1893. This and the following poems are from *Chosen
Poems—A Selection from My Books* (1935).

So sweet, so fleet, so goddess-pure is she.
Her voice is like deep rivers, as they flow
    Through forests bending low.
Her step is softest moonlight, strong to force
    The ocean to its course.
Gentle her smile, for something in man's face,
World-worn, time-weary, furrowed deep with tears,
Thrills her chaste heart with a more tender grace.
Softly she smooths the wrinkles from his brow
    Lined by the baleful years,
Smiles sunshine on the hoar head, whispers low
New charges from the awakened will of Truth—
Words all of fire, that thrill his soul with youth.
Not with his brother is man's battle here;
The challenge of the earth, that Adam heard,
His love austere breathes in his eager ear.
And so the knight who had warred at his king's command,
And scarred the face of Europe, sheathes his sword,
Hearing from untaught lips a nobler word,
Taking new weapons from an unstained hand.
With axe and oar, with mallet and with spade,
She bids the hero conquer, unafraid
Though cloud-veiled Titans be his lordly foes—
Spirits of earth and air, whose wars brook no repose.

    For from far-away mountain and plain,
        From the shores of the sunset sea,
    The unwearying rulers complain, complain,
    And throng from the wastes to defend their reign,
        Their threatened majesty.
    The prairies that lie abloom
        Sigh out to the summer air:
    Shall our dark soil be the tomb
        Of the flowers that rise so fair?
    Shall we yield to man's disdain,
    And nourish his golden grain?
    We will freeze and burn and snare—

        .   .   .   .

Through shining halls a shadowy cavalcade
Of heroes moves on unresounding floors —
Men whose brawned arms upraised these columns high,
And reared the towers that vanish in the sky —
The strong who, having wrought, can never die.

And here, leading a bannered host, comes one
Who held a warring nation in his heart;
Who knew love's agony, but had no part
In love's delight; whose mighty task was done
Through blood and tears that we might walk in joy,
And this day's rapture own no sad alloy.
Around him heirs of bliss, whose bright brows wear
Palm-leaves amid their laurels ever fair.
    Gaily they come, as though the drum
Beat out the call their glad hearts knew so well.
    Brothers once more, dear as of yore,
Who in a noble conflict nobly fell.
Their blood washed pure our banner in the sky.
And quenched the brands under these arches high —
The brave who, having fought, can never die.

Then surging through the vastness rise once more
The aureoled heirs of light, who onward bore
Through darksome times and trackless realms of ruth
The flag of beauty and the torch of truth.
They tore the mask from the foul face of wrong;
To towering mysteries they dared aspire;
High in the choir they built our altar-fire,
And filled these aisles with color and with song:
The ever-young, the unfallen, wreathing for time
Fresh garlands of the seeming-vanished years;
Faces long luminous, remote, sublime,
And shining brows still dewy with our tears.
Back with the old glad smile comes one we knew —

We bade him rear our house of joy today;
But Beauty opened wide her starry way,
And he passed on. Bright champions of the true,
Soldiers of peace, seers, singers ever blest —
From the wide ether of a loftier quest
Their winged souls throng our rites to glorify —
The wise who, having known, can never die.

Strange splendors stream the vaulted aisles along—
To these we loved celestial rapture clings.
And music, borne on rhythm of rising wings,
Floats from the living dead, whose breath is song.

Columbia, my country, dost thou hear?
Ah! dost thou hear the songs unheard of time?
Hark! for their passion trembles at thy ear.
Hush! for thy soul must heed their call sublime.
Across wide seas, unswept by earthly sails,
Those strange sounds draw thee on, for thou shalt be
Leader of nations through the autumnal gales
That wait to mock the strong and wreck the free.
    Dearer, more radiant than of yore,
    Against the dark I see thee rise;
    Thy young smile spurns the guarded shore
    And braves the shadowed ominous skies.
    And still that conquering smile who see
    Pledge love, life, service all to thee.
    The years have brought thee robes most fair—
      The rich processional years—
    And filleted thy shining hair,
    And zoned thy waist with jewels rare,
      And whispered in thy ears
    Strange secrets of God's wondrous ways,
    Long hid from human awe and praise.

Nancy Hanks

Prairie child,
    Brief as dew,
What winds of wonder
    Nourished you?

Rolling plains
    Of billowy green,
Far horizons,
    Blue, serene;

Lofty skies
    The slow clouds climb,
Where burning stars
    Beat out the time:

These, and the dreams
    Of fathers bold,
Baffled longings,
    Hopes untold,

Gave to you
    A heart of fire,
Love like deep waters,
    Brave desire.

Ah, when youth's rapture
    Went out in pain,
And all seemed over,
    Was all in vain?

O soul obscure,
    Whose wings life bound,
And soft death folded
    Under the ground;

Wilding lady,
    Still and true,
Who gave us Lincoln
    And never knew:
To you at last
    Our praise, our tears,
Love and a song
    Through the nation's years!

Mother of Lincoln,
    Our tears, our praise;
A battle-flag
    And the victor's bays!

A Power-Plant

The invisible wheels turn softly round and round—
Light is the tread of brazen-footed Power.
Spirits of air, caged in the iron tower,
Sing as they labor with a purring sound.
The abysmal fires, grated and chained and bound,
Burn white and still, in swift obedience cower;
While far and wide the myriad lamps, a-flower,
Glow like star-gardens and the night confound.
This we have done for you, almighty Lord;
Yes, even as they who built at your command
The pillared temple, or in marble made
Your image, or who sang your deathless word.
We take the weapons of your dread right hand,
And wield them in your service unafraid.

An Ode in Time of Hesitation *

*(After seeing at Boston the Statue of Robert Gould Shaw,
killed while storming Fort Wagner, July 18, 1863, at the
head of the first enlisted Negro regiment, the Fifty-
fourth Massachusetts.)*

I

Before the solemn bronze Saint Gaudens made
To thrill the heedless passer's heart with awe,
And set here in the city's talk and trade
To the good memory of Robert Shaw,
This bright March morn I stand,
And hear the distant spring come up the land;
Knowing that what I hear is not unheard
Of this boy soldier and his Negro band,
For all their gaze is fixed so stern ahead,
For all the fatal rhythm of their tread.
The land they died to save from death and shame
Trembles and waits, hearing the spring's great name,
And by her pangs these resolute ghosts are stirred.

II

Through street and mall the tides of people go
Heedless; the trees upon the Common show
No hint of green; but to my listening heart
The still earth doth impart
Assurance of her jubilant emprise,
And it is clear to my long-searching eyes
That love at last has might upon the skies.
The ice is runneled on the little pond;
A telltale patter drips from off the trees;
The air is touched with southland spiceries,
As if but yesterday it tossed the frond

* This and the poems following are from *Poems and Poetic Dramas,* Vol. I of
The Poems and Plays of William Vaughn Moody (1912), 2 vols.

Of pendant mosses where the live-oaks grow
Beyond Virginia and the Carolines,
Or had its will among the fruits and vines
Of aromatic isles asleep beyond
Florida and the Gulf of Mexico

III

Soon shall the Cape Ann children shout in glee,
Spying the arbutus, spring's dear recluse;
Hill lads at dawn shall hearken the wild goose
Go honking northward over Tennessee;
West from Oswego to Sault Sainte-Marie,
And on to where the Pictured Rocks are hung,
And yonder where, gigantic, wilful, young,
Chicago sitteth at the northwest gates,
With restless violent hands and casual tongue
Moulding her mighty fates,
The Lakes shall robe them in ethereal sheen;
And like a larger sea, the vital green
Of springing wheat shall vastly be outflung
Over Dakota and the prairie states.
By desert people immemorial
On Arizonan mesas shall be done
Dim rites unto the thunder and the sun;
Nor shall the primal gods lack sacrifice
More splendid, when the white Sierras call
Unto the Rockies straightway to arise
And dance before the unveiled ark of the year,
Sounding their windy cedars as for shawms,
Unrolling rivers clear
For flutter of broad phylacteries;
While Shasta signals to Alaskan seas
That watch old sluggish glaciers downward creep
To fling their icebergs thundering from the steep,
And Mariposa through the purple calms
Gazes at far Hawaii crowned with palms
Where East and West are met, —
A rich seal on the ocean's bosom set
To say that East and West are twain,
With different loss and gain:
The Lord hath sundered them; let them be sundered yet.

IV

Alas! what sounds are these that come
Sullenly over the Pacific seas, —
Sounds of ignoble battle, striking dumb
The season's half-awakened ecstasies?
Must I be humble, then,
Now when my heart hath need of pride?
Wild love falls on me from these sculptured men;
By loving much the land for which they died
I would be justified.
My spirit was away on pinions wide
To soothe in praise of her its passionate mood
And ease it of its ache of gratitude.
Too sorely heavy is the debt they lay
On me and the companions of my day.
I would remember now
My country's goodliness, make sweet her name.
Alas! what shade art thou
Of sorrow or of blame
Liftest the lyric leafage from her brow,
And pointest a slow finger at her shame?

V

Lies! lies! It cannot be! The wars we wage
Are noble, and our battles still are won
By justice for us, ere we lift the gage.
We have not sold our loftiest heritage.
The proud republic hath not stopped to cheat
And scramble in the market-place of war;
Her forehead weareth yet its solemn star.
Here is her witness: this, her perfect son,
This delicate and proud New England soul
Who leads despisèd men, with just-unshackled feet,
Up the large ways where death and glory meet,
To show all peoples that our shame is done,
That once more we are clean and spirit-whole.

VI

Crouched in the sea fog on the moaning sand
All night he lay, speaking some simple word

From hour to hour to the slow minds that heard,
Holding each poor life gently in his hand
And breathing on the base rejected clay
Till each dark face shone mystical and grand
Against the breaking day;
And lo, the shard the potter cast away
Was grown a fiery chalice crystal-fine
Fulfilled of the divine
Great wine of battle wrath by God's ring-finger stirred.
Then upward, where the shadowy bastion loomed
Huge on the mountain in the wet sea light,
Whence now, and now, infernal flowerage bloomed,
Bloomed, burst, and scattered down its deadly seed, —
They swept, and died like freemen on the height,
Like freemen, and like men of noble breed;
And when the battle fell away at night
By hasty and contemptuous hands were thrust
Obscurely in a common grave with him
The fair-haired keeper of their love and trust.
Now limb doth mingle with dissolvèd limb
In nature's busy old democracy
To flush the mountain laurel when she blows
Sweet by the southern sea,
And heart with crumbled heart climbs in the rose: —
The untaught hearts with the high heart that knew
This mountain fortress for no earthly hold
Of temporal quarrel, but the bastion old
Of spiritual wrong,
Built by an unjust nation sheer and strong,
Expugnable but by a nation's rue
And bowing down before that equal shrine
By all men held divine,
Whereof his band and he were the most holy sign.

VII

O bitter, bitter shade!
Wilt thou not put the scorn
And instant tragic questions from thine eye?
Do thy dark brows yet crave
That swift and angry stave—
Unmeet for this desirous morn—
That I have striven, striven to evade?

Gazing on him, must I not deem they err
Whose careless lips in street and shop aver
As common tidings, deeds to make his cheek
Flush from the bronze, and his dead throat to speak?
Surely some elder singer would arise,
Whose harp hath leave to threaten and to mourn
Above this people when they go astray.
Is Whitman, the strong spirit, overworn?
Has Whittier put his yearning wrath away?
I will not and I dare not yet believe!
Though furtively the sunlight seems to grieve,
And the spring-laden breeze
Out of the gladdening west is sinister
With sounds of nameless battle overseas;
Though when we turn and question in suspense
If these things be indeed after these ways,
And what things are to follow after these,
Our fluent men of place and consequence
Fumble and fill their mouths with hollow phrase,
Or for the end-all of deep arguments
Intone their dull commercial liturgies —
I dare not yet believe! My ears are shut!
I will not hear the thin satiric praise
And muffled laughter of our enemies,
Bidding us never sheathe our valiant sword
Till we have changed our birthright for a gourd
Of wild pulse stolen from a barbarian's hut;
Showing how wise it is to cast away
The symbols of our spiritual sway,
That so our hands with better ease
May wield the driver's whip and grasp the jailer's keys.

VIII

Was it for this our fathers kept the law?
This crown shall crown their struggle and their ruth?
Are we the eagle nation Milton saw
Mewing its mighty youth,
Soon to possess the mountain winds of truth,
And be a swift familiar of the sun
Where aye before God's face his trumpets run?
Or have we but the talons and the maw,
And for the abject likeness of our heart

Shall some less lordly bird be set apart? —
Some gross-billed wader where the swamps are fat?
Some gorger in the sun? Some prowler with the bat?

IX

Ah no!
We have not fallen so.
We are our fathers' sons: let those who lead us know!
'T was only yesterday sick Cuba's cry
Came up the tropic wind, "Now help us, for we die!"
Then Alabama heard,
And rising, pale, to Maine and Idaho
Shouted a burning word.
Proud state with proud impassioned state conferred,
And at the lifting of a hand sprang forth,
East, west, and south, and north,
Beautiful armies. Oh, by the sweet blood and young
Shed on the awful hill slope at San Juan,
By the unforgotten names of eager boys
Who might have tasted girls' love and been stung
With the old mystic joys
And starry griefs, now the spring nights come on,
But that the heart of youth is generous, —
We charge you, ye who lead us,
Breathe on their chivalry no hint of stain!
Turn not their new-world victories to gain!
One least leaf plucked for chaffer from the bays
Of their dear praise,
One jot of their pure conquest put to hire,
The implacable republic will require;
With clamor, in the glare and gaze of noon,
Or subtly, coming as a thief at night,
But surely, very surely, slow or soon
That insult deep we deeply will requite.
Tempt not our weakness, our cupidity!
For save we let the island men go free,
Those baffled and dislaureled ghosts
Will curse us from the lamentable coasts
Where walk the frustrate dead.
The cup of trembling shall be drained quite,
Eaten the sour bread of astonishment,
With ashes of the hearth shall be made white

Our hair, and wailing shall be in the tent;
Then on your guiltier head
Shall our intolerable self-disdain
Wreak suddenly its anger and its pain;
For manifest in that disastrous light
We shall discern the right
And do it, tardily.—O ye who lead,
Take heed!
Blindness we may forgive, but baseness we will smite.

On a Soldier Fallen in the Philippines

Streets of the roaring town,
Hush for him, hush, be still!
He comes, who was stricken down
Doing the word of our will.
Hush! Let him have his state,
Give him his soldier's crown.
The grists of trade can wait
Their grinding at the mill,
But he cannot wait for his honor, now the trumpet
    has been blown;
Wreathe pride now for his granite brow, lay love
    on his breast of stone.

Toll! Let the great bells toll
Till the clashing air is dim.
Did we wrong this parted soul?
We will make up it to him.
Toll! Let him never guess
What work we set him to.
Laurel, laurel, yes;
He did what we bade him do.
Praise, and never a whispered hint but the fight
    he fought was good;
Never a word that the blood on his sword was
    his country's own heart's-blood.

A flag for the soldier's bier
Who dies that his land may live;
O, banners, banners here,
That he doubt not nor misgive!

That he heed not from the tomb
The evil days draw near
When the nation, robed in gloom,
With its faithless past shall strive.
Let him never dream that his bullet's scream
    went wide of its island mark,
Home to the heart of his darling land where she
    stumbled and sinned in the dark.

The Quarry

Between the rice swamps and the fields of tea
I met a sacred elephant, snow-white.
Upon his back a huge pagoda towered
Full of brass gods and food of sacrifice.
Upon his forehead sat a golden throne,
The massy metal twisted into shapes
Grotesque, antediluvian, such as move
In myth or have their broken images
Sealed in the stony middle of the hills.
A peacock spread his thousand dyes to screen
The yellow sunlight from the head of one
Who sat upon the throne, clad stiff with gems,
Heirlooms of dynasties of buried kings,—
Himself the likeness of a buried king,
With frozen gesture and unfocused eyes.
The trappings of the beast were over-scrawled
With broideries—sea-shapes and flying things,
Fan-trees and dwarfed nodosities of pine,
Mixed with old alphabets, and faded lore
Fallen from ecstatic mouths before the Flood,
Or gathered by the daughters when they walked
Eastward in Eden with the Sons of God
Whom love and the deep moon made garrulous.
Between the carven tusks his trunk hung dead;
Blind as the eyes of pearl in Buddha's brow
His beaded eyes stared thwart upon the road;
And feebler than the doting knees of eld,
His joints, of size to swing the builder's crane
Across the war-walls of the Anakim,
Made vain and shaken haste. Good need was his
To hasten: panting, foaming, on the slot

Came many brutes of prey, their several hates
Laid by until the sharing of the spoil.
Just as they gathered stomach for the leap,
The sun was darkened, and wide-balanced wings
Beat downward on the trade-wind from the sea.
A wheel of shadow sped along the fields
And o'er the dreaming cities. Suddenly
My heart misgave me, and I cried aloud,
"Alas! What dost thou here? What dost *thou* here?"
The great beasts and the little halted sharp,
Eyed the grand circler, doubting his intent.
Straightway the wind flawed and he came about,
Stooping to take the vanward of the pack;
Then turned, between the chasers and the chased,
Crying a word I could not understand, —
But stiller-tongued, with eyes somewhat askance,
They settled to the slot and disappeared.

The Jew to Jesus *

O man of my own people, I alone
Among these alien ones can know thy face,
I who have felt the kinship of our race
Burn in me as I sit where they intone
Thy praises,—those who, striving to make known
A God for sacrifice, have missed the grace
Of thy sweet human meaning in its place,
Thou who art of our blood-bond and our own.

Are we not sharers of thy Passion? Yea,
In spirit-anguish closely by thy side
We have drained the bitter cup, and, tortured, felt
With thee the bruising of each heavy welt.
In every land is our Gethsemane.
A thousand times have we been crucified.

A Girl Strike-Leader

A white-faced, stubborn little thing
Whose years are not quite twenty years,
Eyes steely now and done with tears,
Mouth scornful of its suffering—

The young mouth!—body virginal
Beneath the cheap, ill-fitting suit,
A bearing quaintly resolute,
A flowering hat, satirical.

A soul that steps to the sound of the fife
And banners waving red to war,
Mystical, knowing scarce wherefore—
A Joan in a modern strife.

* The title poem of the 1915 volume from which the following poems by Mrs.
Frank are taken.

The Lake

By the side of my city lies the lake, the large, spreading lake, myriad-
minded.
It knows all thoughts and all passions and has resolved them and
made them one with itself and its vastness.
It knows the shame of the city and its filth; it knows its glory, bright
and burning as a sunrise.
It knows its infinite lassitude and its infinite effort—the gray pall
of futility and the surge and break of the waves of life, pushing
they know not wherefore.
The lake answers all and answers nothing, and is as eternity is,
spreading vast and quiet by the shores of conscious existence.

Sonnet

(*Written for the Lincoln Day celebration of a Chicago
Settlement.*)

What answer shall we make to them that seek
The living vision on a distant shore?
What word of life? The nations at our door,
Believing, cry, "America shall speak!"
We are the strong to succour them the weak,
We are the healers who shall health restore,
Dear God! where our own tides of conflict pour,
Who shall be heard above the din and shriek?

Who, brothers? There was one stood undismayed
'Mid broil of battle and the rancorous strife,
Searching with pitiful eyes the souls of men.
Our martyr calls you, wants you! Now, as then,
The oppressed shall hear him and be not afraid;
And Lincoln dead shall lead you unto life!

A City Equinoctial *

The city mists lie dreaming. From afar
Over the sea of roof-tops veiled and hoar
And hung with sapphire lights, the brumal wind,
The rains transpirant break the clouds to stream
On tenement and ware-house, wharf and spire.

The buoy-lights throb. Fog-horns bay. Athwart
Black shaft and chimney pillared in the smoke,
Past high-splashed walls, past corniced street, swart alley
On crane and shack, the rain swings, beautiful—
Oh, beautiful, thrilled with the brumal wind,
Wind of the night, crying full, full and deep
Resurgent from afar.

                    By rain-whipped roads
By whistling tree, over the wheat-fields bare,
The broken cane, South, North and East and West,
On bayou, swale, lake, mountain-top and valley
Runs the great storm: Tonight, tonight
Past countless house-walls down this very street
Of my own life it courses—storm of the gulf
Storm of the terraced lakes, the ocean shores
Reverberant afar—wind of the world.

Cry, cry again, great voice,
Voice of the hungry storm,
Cry full and far in beauty. For till now
I never heard your cool-spaced, ragged chords
Break on the city house-tops so profoundly—
Welling and coursing from undying springs,
Pure, pure and deep from countless wells and springs—
The tone of striving, the clear tone of tears
Inevitable—voice of the surgent world,

* This and the following poems are from *The Wind in the Corn* (1917).

The speech of disappointments and desires,
Voice of the urgent world, full, full and deep,
The voice of mortal hungers.

More responsive,
Richly responsive and more beautiful
To me the rain, the wind, the night that tell
Over my country's wide-spread plains and towns
Along a thousand cities' towers and lights,
The strength aspirant of the longing earth,
Than all the high ecstatic hymns and harps
Of an envisioned heaven. Till I heard
Fate, death, desire speak deep for all men, heard
From springs unknown the far, clear tone of tears
Inevitable, from unfathomed keeps,
I could not know nor dream of beauty—hark
To the great broken music of the world,
The hungry storm.
Cry, cry again quick voice, across this street,
My life—
Wind of the world, storm of the world, my world,
On unremembering nights blow back, as now
You cry down corniced street and swart-splashed alley,
Over a thousand cities' spires and lights,
The singing prairie brown-spread, plain and free,
Up from the Gulf, up from the ocean shores,
Resurgent from afar.

Lake Winds

Keen, fleet and cool, on your silver-breathed way,
    Whirling the cirrus-cloud, brushing the mire,
Far down the roads of the night and the day,
    Sing me the name of my proudest desire.

Midland wind, inland wind, buoying low,
    Flying on Michigan's gray-dappled deep,
Swing me the strength and the splendor you know
    Once, ere the hour of my infinite sleep.

Fling them but once to me — once let me go
   Straight to some goal through all mist or all mire,
Knowing no thought but to live, as you blow,
   Free in the name of my proudest desire.

To a City Swallow

Over the height of the house-top sea, silver and blue and gray,
A swallow flies, in my city skies, and cries of my city May.

Up from the South, swallow, fly to the North, over the roof-top miles,
The pillaring stacks, and the steam-cloud racks, and the telegraph's
          argent files,
Rich man's and poor man's and beggarman's town, odors of pine and
          pitch,
Marbles and chalk on the hop-scotch walk, and racketing rail and
          switch,
Over a thousand close-housed streets with a million steps arow,
Where the nurses walk and the children talk and the light-gowned
          women go —
Dock-roof, and dive-roof, and prison-house-roof, pebbled and buff and
          brown.
Cry me the manifold souls' abodes, and the roads of my trading town.
For more to me is my house-top sea, where your hooked wings fall and
          soar,
Than all of the echoes you trail for me of your Spring on a woodland
          shore.
Oh, care-free, you flew to the crocused North, when the breath of the
          first Spring woke,
And not of the ways of the jasmine far, but the hours that are, you
          spoke;
And, free, as you flew to the melting North, a myriad Springs ago,
A myriad more, and a myriad more will buoy you swift from the snow,
To cry of the stir of the hours that are, as you cry through my day to
          me —
Through the amethyst of the bright-whirled mist, over a roof-top sea,
Where some window will open, afar, afar, and some woman look out
          and say,
"A swallow flies in my city skies and cries of my city May."

City Vespers

Come home, my child, come home. The fogs are falling:
Along the blue-walled street the whistles calling:
Along the street ten thousand footsteps falling,
    Through steam and smoke-wreath's foam.
Bells cry afar: afar the darkness winging,
Soars throbbing with the chimes and whistles ringing,
The breath of night, the twilight city, singing:
    Come home, my child, come home.

Lock fast the locks, drop down the shutters shading,
From shop and counter, counting-house and trading,
From dock-yard, stock-yard, derrick, crane, and lading,
    From caisson, clay, and loam,
Come home, my child, come home, in many-chording
And rushing voice, the city sings, from hoarding,
From spending, grudging, judging, and recording,
    Come home, my child, come home.

Come from disgrace and honor, craft and scheming,
From work and shirking come, from deed and dreaming,
Success and failure where the lights are streaming
    Azure and chrysolite,
Yellow and crystal, where the mists are falling,
The yard-bells ringing, engine whistles calling,
Along the street ten thousand footsteps falling
    Come through the dark-blown night.

Where tall-piled height and dusky cornice lower
On storied citadel and tall-crowned tower,
Corner and curb a million arc-lights flower
    Full in the twilight air.
If all the foot-falls spoke the destinations
Of all the dreams of all the generations
Upon their way, all shames, all aspirations
    Would find their kindred there.

Here steps your fate, my child, your generation
That walks through time to some far consummation
Unknown along the blue street's destination
    Through fog and smoke-wreath's foam.
Here flies your life, for worse or better winging
And praising with the bells and whistles ringing,
The heart of night, the full-thronged city singing:
    Come home, my child, come home.

3. NEW DIRECTIONS
AND
NEW CONVENTIONS

BECAUSE the year 1912 was marked by such indicative literary events as the establishment by Harriet Monroe of *Poetry: A Magazine of Verse* in Chicago and the publication of Mitchell Kennerley's *The Lyric Year,* it has been traditionally considered the starting point of the American poetic renascence. And if the second decade of the century, to broaden the time a bit, brought a resurgence of American poetry as a whole, it was more than equally a significant time for Illinois: the state now becomes a place of national importance in poetry. Much of the poetry written in Illinois during the quarter century following 1915 reveals a definite freshness in subject matter, spirit, and in form, this last including the results of experimentation in free verse. Though, as we have seen, a poetic maturing had already begun, it was certainly in this period that Illinois experienced its most important production of poetry up to this time, both in amount and in quality. The new poetic attitudes and patterns, however, soon became established and generally resisted further change. It is interesting to note, for example, how little this Illinois poetry, as time goes on, seems touched by the later and new influence of T. S. Eliot; however, one finds in a number of poems a peculiar kind of freshness that might be attributed to the increasing presence of Frost.

To indicate a given year—1940—as the close of this period is not, of course, to assert that this is a clear terminus, for a number of the poets who began writing in these years continued well beyond that date. The choice of poets, then, in this section has been made from those who achieved basic recognition, temporary or more lasting, within the period indicated; and the dates of only a few poems—for example, several of Van Doren's—fall beyond 1940. Finally it should be stated that under the pressure of space limitations a number of borderline Illinois poets have not been included, "borderline" meaning that although these poets had a real connection with Illinois (some with the Poetry Club at the University of Chicago), their most significant linkage or that of their poetry is with some other state or region. This can be said of such poets as Lew Sarett, Alice Corbin, Janet Lewis, Yvor Winters, and Glenway Wescott.

As the productive periods of the poets included overlap and vary considerably in length, the sequence in which they are presented here is only loosely chronological, and is conditioned by other considerations, such as their relationship to a given place or to each other. As was true of some of the other poets, Eunice Tietjens and Maxwell Bodenheim were involved in the Chicago poetic activity of the very early years of this period. The involvement of the former included not only the publication of her own writing, but also work on the staff of *Poetry* for a number of years beginning in 1913. Bodenheim came as a young man to Illinois in 1914, and though he went on later to establish himself elsewhere, the Illinois connection is significant, for he wrote some of his most interesting poetry in and concerning Chicago. It is logical to consider Masters, Lindsay, and Sandburg together, although the poetry of Sandburg, because of his poetic longevity, is placed rather late in the present section. These three, certainly the best known of the twentieth-century Illinois poets, are usually considered a part of the "Chicago School"; nevertheless, their poetic expression, as witnessed by their poems in this volume, reveals a small town and rural Illinois conditioning. By 1915 all three had published some important poetry, and they continued, with success rather unevenly divided among them, in the years to follow. Each is very much an Illinois poet, yet at this time, 1968, shortly after the death of Sandburg, special tribute might suitably be offered to him as a poetic embodiment of the state, which for Sandburg might well be called Lincoln's state.

The remaining poets in this part of the anthology were variously connected with Illinois and reflect these connections in individual ways. Marjorie Seiffert lived in Moline and in Chicago, where in 1916, to mention an extracurricular item, she joined with Witter Bynner and Arthur Ficke in perpetrating the *Spectra* hoax, the satire on the Imagists. The poetry of Mark Turbyfill clearly echoes the Illinois of his experience—Chicago, from the time that the poet was fourteen. Biographically, and to a great extent poetically, Marion Strobel is almost all Chicago; here in this city she was one of that considerable number of Illinois poets who early or late made an additional contribution by their editorial work on *Poetry*. George Dillon was still another, and one whose poetic successes as an undergraduate at the University of Chicago were publicly validated some years later when, in 1931, *The Flowering Stone* brought him the Pulitzer Prize for Poetry. The early Illinois years of Glenn Ward Dresbach and, after a considerable sojourn out of the state, a number of his later years in rural Illinois and the shorter time spent in Chicago are reflected in many of his poems. Jessica Nelson North, born in Wisconsin, arrived poetically in Chicago, where she, too, was active on the staff of *Poetry* from 1927 to 1929, and where she continued to live and write. Paul Scott Mowrer and Mark Van Doren are two poets who, though they were removed physically from Illinois by occupational circumstances, reveal in a moving way the intangible ties binding them to the place of their earlier years. Mowrer was born in Bloomington and later, after a short time as a Chicago reporter, spent most of his years as a foreign correspondent and editor and now lives in New England. Van Doren was born in Hope, Illinois, and after receiving his A.B. and M.A. from the University of Illinois and his Ph.D. from Columbia was for many years professor of English at that latter University. Very clearly the major poetic connections for both were with their native state.

Transcontinental *

The train spins forward endlessly.
Outside
The sunlit trees and the patient procreant fields
Flash past me and are gone.
Drab little houses pass me silently,
Colored without from the drab lives within.

I see them, and I see them not.
My heart
Half dwells behind me, lingering with lips new-lost,
And half leaps forward to the journey's end.
Only my body sits here listlessly,
Here where the sunlit trees
Flash past me and are gone.

The Drug Clerk

The drug clerk stands behind the counter,
Young and dapper, debonair . . .

Before him burn the great unwinking lights,
The hectic stars of city nights,
Red as hell's pit, green as a mermaid's hair.
A queer half acrid smell is in the air.
Behind him on the shelves in ordered rows
With strange abbreviated names
Dwell half the facts of life. That young man knows
Bottled and boxed and powdered here
Dumb tragedies, deceptions, secret shames,
And comedy, and fear.

Sleep slumbers here, like a great quiet sea
Shrunk to this bottle's compass, sleep that brings

* This and the two poems following are from *Body and Raiment* (1919).

Sweet respite from the teeth of pain
To those poor tossing things
That the white nurses watch so thoughtfully.
And here again
Dwell the shy souls of Maytime flowers
That shall make sweeter still those poignant hours
When wide-eyed youth looks on the face of love.
And, for those others who have found too late
The bitter fruit thereof,
Here are cosmetics, powders, paints—the arts
That hunted women use to hunt again
With scented flesh for bait.
And here is comfort for the hearts
Of sucking babes in their first teething pain.
Here dwells the substance of huge fervid dreams,
Fantastic, many-colored, shot with gleams
Of ecstasy and madness, that shall come
To some pale twitching sleeper in a bunk.
And here is courage, cheaply bought
To cure a sick blue funk,
And dearly paid for in the final sum.
Here in this powdered fly is caught
Desire more ravishing than Tarquin's, rape
And bloody-handed murder. And at last
When the one weary hope is past
Here is the sole escape,
The little postern in the house of breath
Where pallid fugitives keep tryst with death.

All this the drug clerk knows, and there he stands,
Young and dapper, debonair . . .
He rests a pair of slender hands,
Much manicured, upon the counter there
And speaks: "No, we don't carry no pomade.
We only cater to the high-class trade."

The Steam Shovel

Beneath my window in a city street
A monster lairs, a creature huge and grim
And only half believed; the strength of him—
Steel strung and fit to meet

The strength of earth—
Is mighty as men's dreams that conquer force.
Steam belches from him. He is the new birth
of old Behemoth, late sprung from the source
Whence Grendel sprang, and all the monster clan
Dead for an age, now born again of man.

The iron head
Set on a monstrous, jointed neck,
Glides here and there, lifts, settles on the red
Moist Floor, with nose dropped in the dirt, at beck
Of some incredible control.
He snorts, and pauses couchant for a space,
Then slowly lifts; and tears the gaping hole
Yet deeper in earth's flank. A sudden race
Of loosened earth and pebbles trickles there
Like blood-drops in a wound.
But he, the monster, swings his load around
Weightless it seems as air. His mammoth jaw
Drops widely opened with a rasping sound
And all the red earth vomits from his maw.

Oh, patient monster, born at man's decree,
A lap-dog dragon, eating from his hand
And doomed to fetch and carry at command,
Have you no longing ever to be free?
In warm electric days to run a-muck,
Ranging like some mad dinosaur,
Your fiery heart at war
With this strange world, the city's restless ruck,
Where all drab things that toil, save you alone,
Have life;
And you the semblance only—and the strife?
Do you not yearn to rip the roots of stone
Of these great piles men build
And hurl them down with shriek of shattered steel,
Scorning your own sure doom, so you may feel,
You too, the lust with which your sires killed?
Or is your soul in very deed so tame,
The blood of Grendel watered to a gruel,
That you are well content
With heart of flame
Thus placidly to chew your cud of fuel

And toil in peace for man's aggrandizement?
Poor helpless creature of a half grown god,
Blind of yourself and impotent!
At night
When your forerunners, sprung from quicker sod,
Ranged through primeval woods, hot on the scent,
Or waked the stars with amorous delight,
You stand, a soiled unwieldy mass of steel,
Black in the arc-light, modern as your name,
Dead and unsouled and trite;
Till I must feel
A quick creator's pity for your shame—
That man who made you and who gave so much
Yet cannot give the last transforming touch,
That with the work he cannot give the wage,
For day, no joy of night,
For toil, no ecstasy of primal rage.

After War *

(*For L. C. B., killed in action.*)

You died then, you and seven million more.
You died for home, or victory, or peace.
These things we have, and life's much as before
Save for the silence where your voices cease,

Save for the human silences that come
When those who loved you suddenly are still
Remembering—or at twilight when the numb
Sore spot in the heart, like an old wound, aches chill.

Life runs the same. The outer shell of living
Which when we lost you covered emptiness
Is deepening now, is taking form, and giving
Solidity to what was bodiless.

Oh, we have not forgotten! We remember.
Yet we have lost the glory of your days.

* This poem and the sonnet following are from *Leaves in Windy Weather* (1929).

Time circles still from spring to stark December
And we slip back into the trodden ways.

Yes, we grow old; and our once naked hearts
That glowed like steel with agony and wrath
Grow dusty with long days, and little arts
And gracious nothings deck the aftermath.

But you are free, who went in that white glow
And laid you down with tragedy for bride.
Life cannot touch you. You can never grow
Old and cold and dusty at our side.

For you are youth, who now have cheated time,
And you are courage flung against the sky,
One with all radiant things that in their prime
Are frozen into beauty when they die.

And death, who had his will of you, can never
Still that high courage with a thousand wars.
And we who love you hold you now forever,
As wide and white and peaceful as the stars.

X

One of thirteen poems in
"From the Mountains—A Sonnet Sequence"

The little ledge of pine and tamarack
Is empty now of all save wind and rain,
For you have gone and I am going back—
Back to the struggling, juggling town again.
The far peaks cluster still, each one a cry,
A frozen note of singing in the sun.
The world that waked me lies unchanged, but I
Am growing weary now that summer's done.
And in my spirit stirs the old unrest
That drives me desolately through the years.
My untuned heart droops slackly in my breast,
And beauty wakes no longer any tears.
Dear mountains, where my soul has breathed so deep,
May snow lie lightly on your winter's sleep!

Fire-Brick *

My fire-bricks as I sit, huddled for warmth,
Say "Stevens" on them now. But I recall
That on Babylonian brick the legend runs
"Nebuchadnezzar," and that Roman brick
And Carthaginian bear the pregnant names
"Caesar" and "Hannibal."

                        For bricks remain.
Bricks still outlast the fire, though they are burnt
First in the fire to hardness. Ever so
The cycle goes, of fire for brick, and brick
For fire, till there shall be no more of fire.

And any name will do, so man be warm.

  * from *Poetry: A Magazine of Verse,* March, 1940.

Advice to a Street-Pavement *

Lacerated grey has bitten
Into your shapeless humility.
Little episodes of roving
Strew their hieroglyphics on your muteness.
Life has given you heavy stains
Like an ointment growing stale.
Endless feet tap over you
With a maniac insistence.

O unresisting street-pavement,
Keep your passive insolence
At the dwarfs who scorn you with their feet.
Only one who lies upon his back
Can disregard the stars.

Advice to a Blue-Bird

Who can make a delicate adventure
Of walking on the ground?
Who can make grass-blades
Arcades for pertly careless straying?
You alone, who skim against these leaves,
Turning all desire into light whips
Moulded by your deep blue wing-tips,
You who shrill your unconcern
Into the sternly antique sky.
You to whom all things
Hold an equal kiss of touch.

Mincing, wanton blue-bird,
Grimace at the hoofs of passing men.
You alone can lose yourself
Within a sky, and rob it of its blue!

* This and the four poems following are from *Advice—A Book of Poems* (1920).

82

Track-Workers

The rails you carry cut into your hands,
Like the sharp lips of an unsought lover.
As you stumble over the ties
Sunlight is clinging, yellow spit
Raining down upon your faces.
You are the living cuspidors of day.
Dirt, its teasing ghost, dust,
And passionless kicks of steel, fill you.
Flowers sprouting near the tracks,
Brush their lightly odoured hands
In vain against your stale jackets of sweat.
Within you, minds and hearts
Are snoring to the curt rhythm of your breath.
You do not see this blustering blackbird
Promenading on a barbed-wire fence.
He eyes you with spritelike hauteur,
Unable to understand
Why your motions endlessly copy each other.
One of you, a meek and burly Pole,
Peers a moment at the strutting blackbird
With a fleeting shade of dull resentment. . . .
There is always one among you
Who recoils from glimpsing corpses.

Advice to a River Steam-Boat

The brass band plays upon your decks,
Like a sturdy harlot aping mirth,
And people in starched shields
Stuff their passions with sweet words,
Life is swishing in the air,
Like a tipsy, unseen bridegroom.

O humbly grunting river boat,
Take the churning water and the sun
Like one who plays with his own chains
And flings their turmoil to the sky.
Only a voice can leap above high walls.

Dialogue Between a Past and Present Poet

PAST POET

I wrote of roses on a woman's breast,
Glowing as though her blood
Had welled out to a spellbound fierceness;
And the glad, light mixture of her hair.
I wrote of God and angels.
They stole the simple blush of my desire
To make their isolated triumph human.
Knights and kings flooded my song,
Catching with their glittering clash
The unheard boldness in my life.
Gods and nymphs slipped through my voice,
And with the lofty scurrying of their feet
Spurned the smirched angers of my days.

PRESENT POET

You raised an unhurried, church-like escape.
You lingered in shimmering idleness;
Or lengthened a prayer into a lance;
Or strengthened a thought till it heaved off all of life
And dropped its sightless heaven into your smile.
Life, to us, is a colourless tangle.
Like madly gorgeous weavers
Our eyes reiterate themselves on life.

PAST POET

My towering simplicity
Loosening an evening of belief
Over the things it dared not view,
Gladly shunned reality
Just as your mad weaver does.

PRESENT POET

Reality is a formless lure,
And only when we know this
Do we dare to be unreal.

The Hill *

Where are Elmer, Herman, Bert, Tom and Charley,
The weak of will, the strong of arm, the clown, the boozer, the
fighter?
All, all, are sleeping on the hill.

One passed in a fever,
One was burned in a mine,
One was killed in a brawl,
One died in a jail,
One fell from a bridge toiling for children and wife—
All, all are sleeping, sleeping, sleeping on the hill.

Where are Ella, Kate, Mag, Lizzie and Edith,
The tender heart, the simple soul, the loud, the proud, the happy
one?—
All, all, are sleeping on the hill.

One died in shameful child-birth,
One of a thwarted love,
One at the hands of a brute in a brothel,
One of a broken pride, in the search for heart's desire,
One after life in far-away London and Paris
Was brought to her little space by Ella and Kate and Mag—
All, all are sleeping, sleeping, sleeping on the hill.

Where are Uncle Isaac and Aunt Emily,
And old Towny Kincaid and Sevigne Houghton,
And Major Walker who had talked
With venerable men of the revolution?—
All, all, are sleeping on the hill.

* from the *Spoon River Anthology* (1915). Following this introductory poem,
seven of the 244 autobiographical epitaphs are presented here.

They brought them dead sons from the war,
And daughters whom life had crushed,
And their children fatherless, crying—
All, all are sleeping, sleeping, sleeping on the hill.

Where is Old Fiddler Jones
Who played with life all his ninety years,
Braving the sleet with bared breast,
Drinking, rioting, thinking neither of wife nor kin,
Nor gold, nor love, nor heaven?
Lo! he babbles of the fish-frys of long ago,
Of the horse-races of long ago at Clary's Grove,
Of what Abe Lincoln said
One time at Springfield.

Hod Putt

Here I lie close to the grave
Of Old Bill Piersol,
Who grew rich trading with the Indians, and who
Afterwards took the bankrupt law
And emerged from it richer than ever.
Myself grown tired of toil and poverty
And beholding how Old Bill and others grew in wealth,
Robbed a traveler one night near Proctor's Grove,
Killing him unwittingly while doing so,
For the which I was tried and hanged.
That was my way of going into bankruptcy.
Now we who took the bankrupt law in our respective ways
Sleep peacefully side by side.

Barney Hainsfeather

If the excursion train to Peoria
Had just been wrecked, I might have escaped with my life—
Certainly I should have escaped this place.
But as it was burned as well, they mistook me
For John Allen who was sent to the Hebrew Cemetery
At Chicago,
And John for me, so I lie here.
It was bad enough to run a clothing store in this town,
But to be buried here—*ach!*

Daisy Fraser

Did you ever hear of Editor Whedon
Giving to the public treasury any of the money he received
For supporting candidates for office?
Or for writing up the canning factory
To get people to invest?
Or for suppressing the facts about the bank,
When it was rotten and ready to break?
Did you ever hear of the Circuit Judge
Helping anyone except the "Q" railroad,
Or the bankers? Or did Rev. Peet or Rev. Sibley
Give any part of their salary, earned by keeping still,
Or speaking out as the leaders wished them to do,
To the building of the water works?
But I—Daisy Fraser who always passed
Along the streets through rows of nods and smiles,
And coughs and words such as "there she goes,"
Never was taken before Justice Arnett
Without contributing ten dollars and costs
To the school fund of Spoon River!

Harry Wilmans

I was just turned twenty-one,
And Henry Phipps, the Sunday-school superintendent,
Made a speech in Bindle's Opera House.
"The honor of the flag must be upheld," he said,
"Whether it be assailed by a barbarous tribe of Tagalogs
Or the greatest power in Europe."
And we cheered and cheered the speech and the flag he waved
As he spoke.
And I went to the war in spite of my father,
And followed the flag till I saw it raised
By our camp in a rice field near Manila,
And all of us cheered and cheered it.
But there were flies and poisonous things;
And there was the deadly water,
And the cruel heat,

And the sickening, putrid food;
And the smell of the trench just back of the tents
Where the soldiers went to empty themselves;
And there were the whores who followed us, full of syphilis;
And beastly acts between ourselves or alone,
With bullying, hatred, degradation among us,
And days of loathing and nights of fear
To the hour of the charge through the steaming swamp,
Following the flag,
Till I fell with a scream, shot through the guts.
Now there's a flag over me in Spoon River!
A flag! A flag!

William H. Herndon

There by the window in the old house
Perched on the bluff, overlooking miles of valley,
My days of labor closed, sitting out life's decline,
Day by day did I look in my memory,
As one who gazes in an enchantress's crystal globe,
And I saw the figures of the past,
As if in a pageant glassed by a shining dream,
Move through the incredible sphere of time.
And I saw a man arise from the soil like a fabled giant
And throw himself over a deathless destiny,
Master of great armies, head of the republic,
Bringing together into a dithyramb of recreative song
The epic hopes of a people;
At the same time Vulcan of sovereign fires,
Where imperishable shields and swords were beaten out
From spirits tempered in heaven.
Look in the crystal! See how he hastens on
To the place where his path comes up to the path
Of a child of Plutarch and Shakespeare.
O Lincoln, actor indeed, playing well your part,
And Booth, who strode in a mimic play within the play.
Often and often I saw you,
As the cawing crows winged their way to the wood
Over my house-top at solemn sunsets,
There by my window,
Alone.

Anne Rutledge

Out of me unworthy and unknown
The vibrations of deathless music;
"With malice toward none, with charity for all."
Out of me the forgiveness of millions toward millions,
And the beneficent face of a nation
Shining with justice and truth.
I am Anne Rutledge who sleep beneath these weeds,
Beloved in life of Abraham Lincoln,
Wedded to him, not through union,
But through separation.
Bloom forever, O Republic,
From the dust of my bosom!

Lucinda Matlock

I went to the dances at Chandlerville,
And played snap-out at Winchester.
One time we changed partners,
Driving home in the moonlight of middle June,
And then I found Davis.
We were married and lived together for seventy years,
Enjoying, working, raising the twelve children,
Eight of whom we lost
Ere I had reached the age of sixty.
I spun, I wove, I kept the house, I nursed the sick,
I made the garden, and for holiday
Rambled over the fields where sang the larks,
And by Spoon River gathering many a shell,
And many a flower and medicinal weed—
Shouting to the wooded hills, singing to the green valleys.
At ninety-six I had lived enough, that is all,
And passed to a sweet repose.
What is this I hear of sorrow and weariness,
Anger, discontent and drooping hopes?
Degenerate sons and daughters,
Life is too strong for you—
It takes life to love Life.

Chicago *

I

On the gray paper of this mist and fog
With dust for the erasure and with smoke
For drawing crayons, be this charcoal scrawl:
The breed of Gog in the kingdom of Magog,
Skyscrapers, helmeted, stand sentinel
Amid the obscuring fumes of coal and coke,
Raised by enchantment out of the sand and bog
This sky-line, the Sierras of the lake,
Cuts with dulled teeth,
Which twist and break,
The imponderable and drifting steam.
And restlessly beneath
This man-created mountain chain,
Like the flow of a prairie river
Endlessly by day and night, forever
Along the boulevards pedestrians stream
In a shuffle like dancers to a low refrain:
Forever by day and night,
Pursuing as of old the lure of delight,
And the ghosts of pleasure or pain.
Their rhythmic feet sound like the falling of rain,
Or the hush of the waves, when the roar
Is blown by a wind off shore.

II

From a tower like a mountain promontory
The cesspool of a railroad lies to view,
Fouling the marble of the city's glory;
A crapulous sluice of garbage and of cars,
Where engines rush and whistle, smudge the blue
With filth like the trail of slugs.
It is a trench of steel which bars
Free access to the common shore, and hugs
In a coil of lazar arms the boulevard.

* from *Starved Rock* (1919).

Cattle and hogs delivered here for slaughter
Corrupt the loveliness of the water front.
They low and grunt,
Switched back and forth within the tangled yard.
But from this tower the amethystine water,
The water of jade or slate,
Is visible with its importunate
Gestures against the sky to still retreats
In Michigan, of quiet woods and hills
Beyond the simmering passion of these streets,
And all their endless ills. . . .

III

But over the switch yard stands the Institute
Guarded by lions on the avenue,
Colossal lions standing for attack;
Between whose feet luminous and resolute
Children of the city passing through
To palettes, compasses, the demoniac
Spirit of the city shall subdue.
Lions are in the loop and jackals too.
They have no trainers but the alderman,
Who uses them to hunt with. But in time
The city shall behold its nobler plan
Achieved by hands that rhyme.
Workers who architect and build,
And out of thought its substance re-arrange,
Till all its prophecies shall be fulfilled.
Through numbers, science and art
The city shall know change,
And win dominion over water and light,
The cyclop's mastery of the mart;
The devils overcome,
Which stalk the squalid ways by night
Of poverty and the slum,
Where the crook is spawned, the burglar and the bum.
These youths who pass the lions shall assuage
The city's thirst and hunger,
And save it from the wastage and the wage
Of the demagogue, the precinct monger.

IV

This is the city of great doges hidden
In guarded offices and country places.
The city strives against the things forbidden
By the doges, on whose faces
The city at large never looks;
Doges who could accomplish if they would
In a month the city's beauty and good.
Yet this city in a hundred years has risen
Out of a haunt of foxes, wolves and rooks,
And breaks asunder now the bars of the prison
Of dead days and dying. It has spread
For many a rood its boundaries, like the sprawled
And fallen Hephaestos, and has tenanted
Its neighborhoods increasing and unwalled
With peoples from all lands.
From Milwaukee Avenue to the populous mills
Of South Chicago, from the Sheridan Drive
Through forests where the water smiles
To Harlem for miles and miles.
It reaches out its hands,
Powerful and alive
With dreams to touch to-morrow, which it wills
To dawn and which shall dawn. . . .
And like lights that twinkle through the stench
And putrid mist of abattoirs,
Great souls are here, separate and withdrawn,
Companionless, whom darkness cannot quench.
Seeing they are the chrysalis which must feed
Upon its own thoughts and the life to be,
Its flight among the stars.
Beauty is here, like half protected flowers,
Blooms and will cast its multiplying seed,
Until one mass of color shall succeed
The shaley places of these arid hours.

Chicago! by this inland sea
In the land of Lincoln, in the State
Of souls who held the nation's fate,
City both old and young, I consecrate

Your future years to truth and liberty.
Be this the record frail and incomplete
Of one who saw you, mingled with the masses
Along these magical mountain passes
With restless yet with hopeful feet.
Could they return to see you who have slept
These fifty years, who laid your first foundations!
And oh! could we behold you who have kept
Their promise for you, when new generations
Shall walk this boulevard made fair
In chiseled marble, looking at the lake
Of clearer water under a bluer air.
We who shall sleep then nor awake,
Have left the labor to you and the care
Ask great fulfillment, for ourselves a prayer!

Illinois Ozarks *

The Ozarks of Illinois extend,
Peaceful and primitive, like an etching study,
From the Mississippi and the Big Muddy
To the Saline and Ohio, where they end.
These hills are rugged, strewn with barren rocks,
But spaced with uplands of pastures green
Where sheep browse in a scene that mocks
White clouds above in a blue serene.

Ridges of woodland toward the horizon space
The pastoral silence, where the West commences,
Dotted by log-cabins, lined with rail fences,
Which change and passing years do not displace.
The past still lingers here, that Illinois
Peopled by Kentucky and by Tennessee,
When life was war-less, happy and free
From the insatiate cities which drain, destroy.

Even as the sky suffers no change, the clouds
Still pause, as even the meditating sheep
With bent heads crop the grass, or sleep
By moonlight, so these hills, remote from crowds

* from *Illinois Poems* (1941).

Where war fanatics ply their poisonous lies,
Retain their beauty, they are the wilderness,
Which is now ere the undergrowth ramifies
The streets of cities, as Chichen Itcha the stress
Of the encroaching jungle felt. These hills will tell
For centuries to come about the land,
About that good America, before the hand
Of hate, corruption turned life into hell.

With Canada on our north, and to our south
Isles close to our River's mouth;
With our Canal in equal ownership
Of Britain, we are a province strip
Surrounded by an enemy, which schemes
To lay in death our leadership,
And take us over, ending all our dreams,
Fulfilling thereby the word of Cecil Rhodes,
And Ruskin, that in time the heavy toil
Of the Revolution should prove an episode's
Meaningless day, and this our sovereign soil
Should once again by England's commerce spoil.

The Illinois Village *

O you who lose the art of hope,
Whose temples seem to shrine a lie,
Whose sidewalks are but stones of fear,
Who weep that Liberty must die,
Turn to the little prairie towns,
Your higher hope shall yet begin.
On every side awaits you there
Some gate where glory enters in.
Yet when I see the flocks of girls,
Watching the Sunday train go thro'
(As tho' the whole wide world went by)
With eyes that long to travel too,
I sigh, despite my soul made glad
By cloudy dresses and brown hair,
Sigh for the sweet life wrenched and torn
By thundering commerce, fierce and bare.
Nymphs of the wheat these girls should be:
Kings of the grove, their lovers, strong.
Why are they not inspired, aflame?
This beauty calls for valiant song —
For men to carve these fairy-forms
And faces in a fountain-frieze;
Dancers that own immortal hours;
Painters that work upon their knees;
Maids, lovers, friends, so deep in life,
So deep in love and poet's deeds,
The railroad is a thing disowned,
The city but a field of weeds.

Who can pass a village church
By night in these clean prairie lands
Without a touch of Spirit-power?
So white and fixed and cool it stands —
A thing from some strange fairy-town,

* This and the following poems, unless otherwise indicated, are from *Collected Poems* (1925).

A pious amaranthine flower,
Unsullied by the winds, as pure
As jade or marble, wrought this hour:
Rural in form, foursquare and plain,
And yet our sister, the new moon,
Makes it a praying wizard's dream.
The trees that watch at dusty noon
Breaking its sharpest lines, veil not
The whiteness it reflects from God,
Flashing like Spring on many an eye,
Making clean flesh, that once was clod.
Who can pass a district school
Without the hope that there may wait
Some baby-heart the books shall flame
With zeal to make his playmates great,
To make the whole wide village gleam
A strangely carved celestial gem,
Eternal in its beauty-light,
The Artist's town of Bethlehem!

The Angel and the Clown

I saw wild domes and bowers
And smoking incense towers
And mad exotic flowers
In Illinois.
Where ragged ditches ran
Now springs of Heaven began
Celestial drink for man
In Illinois.

There stood beside the town
Beneath its incense-crown
An angel and a clown
In Illinois.
He was as Clowns are:
She was snow and star
With eyes that looked afar
In Illinois.

I asked, "How came this place
Of antique Asian grace

Amid our callow race
In Illinois?"
Said Clown and Angel fair:
"By laughter and by prayer,
By casting off all care
In Illinois."

Factory Windows are Always Broken

Factory windows are always broken.
Somebody's always throwing bricks,
Somebody's always heaving cinders,
Playing ugly Yahoo tricks.

Factory windows are always broken.
Other windows are let alone.
No one throws through the chapel-window
The bitter, snarling, derisive stone.

Factory windows are always broken.
Something or other is going wrong.
Something is rotten—I think, in Denmark.
End of the factory-window song.

Why I voted the Socialist Ticket

I am unjust, but I can strive for justice.
My life's unkind, but I can vote for kindness.
I, the unloving, say life should be lovely.
I, that am blind, cry out against my blindness.

Man is a curious brute—he pets his fancies—
Fighting mankind, to win sweet luxury.
So he will be, tho' law be clear as crystal,
Tho' all men plan to live in harmony.

Come let us vote against our human nature,
Crying to God in all the polling places
To heal our everlasting sinfulness
And make us sages with transfigured faces.

Nancy Hanks, Mother of Abraham Lincoln *

"Out of the eater came forth meat; and out of the strong
came forth Sweetness." Judges 14:14

A sweet girl graduate, lean as a fawn,
The very whimsy of time,
Read her class upon Commencement Day—
A trembling filigree rhyme.
The pansy that blooms on the window sill,
Blooms in exactly the proper place;
And she nodded just like a pansy there,
And her poem was all about bowers and showers,
Sugary streamlet and mossy rill,
All about daisies on dale and hill—
And she was the mother of Buffalo Bill.

Another girl, a cloud-drift sort,
Dreamlit, moonlit, marble-white,
Light-footed saint on the pilgrim shore,
The best since New England fairies began,
Was the mother of Barnum, the circus man
A girl from Missouri, snippy and vain,
As frothy a miss as any you know,
A wren, a toy, a pink silk bow,
The belle of the choir, she drove insane
Missouri deacons and all the sleek,
Her utter tomfoolery made man weak,
Till they could not stand and they could not speak.
Oh, queen of fifteen and sixteen,
Missouri sweetened beneath her reign—
And she was the mother of bad Mark Twain.

Not always are lions born of lions,
Roosevelt sprang from a palace of lace;
On the other hand is the dizzy truth:
Not always is beauty born of beauty.
Some treasures wait in a hidden place.
All over the world were thousands of belles.
In far-off eighteen hundred and nine,

* from *Going-To-The-Stars* (1926).

Girls, of fifteen, girls of twenty,
Their mamas dressed them up a-plenty—
Each garter was bright, each stocking fine,
But for all their innocent devices,
Their cheeks of fruit and their eyes of wine,
And each voluptuous design,
And all soft glories that we trace
In Europe's palaces of lace,
A girl who slept in dust and sorrow,
Nancy Hanks, in a lost cabin,
Nancy Hanks had the loveliest face!

Abraham Lincoln Walks at Midnight

(*In Springfield, Illinois*)

It is portentous, and a thing of state
That here at midnight, in our little town
A mourning figure walks, and will not rest,
Near the old court-house pacing up and down,

Or by his homestead, or in shadowed yards
He lingers where his children used to play,
Or through the market, on the well-worn stones
He stalks until the dawn-stars burn away.

A bronzed, lank man! His suit of ancient black,
A famous high top-hat and plain worn shawl
Make him the quaint great figure that men love,
The prairie-lawyer, master of us all.

He cannot sleep upon his hillside now.
He is among us: —as in times before!
And we who toss and lie awake for long,
Breathe deep, and start, to see him pass the door.

His head is bowed. He thinks of men and kings.
Yea, when the sick world cries, how can he sleep?
Too many peasants fight, they know not why;
Too many homesteads in black terror weep.

The sins of all the war-lords burn his heart.
He sees the dreadnaughts scouring every main.
He carries on his shawl-wrapped shoulders now
The bitterness, the folly and the pain.

He cannot rest until a spirit-dawn
Shall come; — the shining hope of Europe free:
A league of sober folk, the workers' earth,
Bringing long peace to Cornland, Alp and Sea.

It breaks his heart that kings must murder still,
That all his hours of travail here for men
Seem yet in vain. And who will bring white peace
That he may sleep upon his hill again?

Lincoln *

Would I might rouse the Lincoln in you all,
That which is gendered in the wilderness
From lonely prairies and God's tenderness.
Imperial soul, star of a weedy stream,
Born where the ghosts of buffaloes still dream,
Whose spirit hoof-beats storm above his grave,
Above that breast of earth and prairie-fire —
Fire that freed the slave.

Bryan, Bryan, Bryan, Bryan

*The Campaign of Eighteen Ninety-six, as Viewed at the
Time By a Sixteen-Year-Old, Etc.*

I

In a nation of one hundred fine, mob-hearted, lynching, relenting,
repenting millions
There are plenty of sweeping, swinging, stinging, gorgeous things to
shout about,
And knock your old blue devils out.

I brag and chant of Bryan, Bryan, Bryan,
Candidate for president who sketched a silver Zion,

* from *General William Booth Enters Into Heaven and Other Poems* (1913).

The one American Poet who could sing outdoors,
He brought in tides of wonder, of unprecedented splendor,
Wild roses from the plains, that made hearts tender,
All the funny circus silks
Of politics unfurled,
Bartlett pears of romance that were honey at the cores,
And torchlights down the street, to the end of the world.

There were truths eternal in the gab and tittle-tattle.
There were real heads broken in the fustian and the rattle.
There were real lines drawn:
Not the silver and the gold,
But Nebraska's cry went eastward against the dour and old,
The mean and cold.

It was eighteen ninety-six, and I was just sixteen
And Altgeld ruled in Springfield, Illinois,
When there came from the sunset Nebraska's shout of joy:
In a coat like a deacon, in a black Stetson hat
He scourged the elephant plutocrats
With barbed wire from the Platte.
The scales dropped from their mighty eyes.
They saw that summer's noon
A tribe of wonders coming
To a marching tune.

Oh, the longhorns from Texas,
The jay hawks from Kansas,
The plop-eyed bungaroo and giant giassicus,
The varmint, chipmunk, bugaboo,
The horned-toad, prairie-dog and ballyhoo,
From all the newborn states arow,
Bidding the eagles of the west fly on,
Bidding the eagles of the west fly on.
The fawn, prodactyl and thing-a-ma-jig,
The rakaboor, the hellangone,
The whangdoodle, batfowl and pig,
The coyote, wild-cat and grizzly in a glow,
In a miracle of health and speed, the whole breed abreast,
They leaped the Mississippi, blue border of the West,
From the Gulf to Canada, two thousand miles long: —
Against the towns of Tubal Cain,
Ah, — sharp was their song.

Against the ways of Tubal Cain, too cunning for the young,
The longhorn calf, the buffalo and wampus gave tongue.

These creatures were defending things Mark Hanna never dreamed:
The moods of airy childhood that in desert dews gleamed,
The gossamers and whimsies,
The monkeyshines and didoes
Rank and strange
Of the canyons and the range,
The ultimate fantastics
Of the far western slope,
And of prairie schooner children
Born beneath the stars,
Beneath falling snows,
Of the babies born at midnight
In the sod huts of lost hope,
With no physician there,
Except a Kansas prayer,
With the Indian raid a howling through the air.

And all these in their helpless days
By the dour East oppressed,
Mean paternalism
Making their mistakes for them,
Crucifying half the West,
Till the whole Atlantic coast
Seemed a giant spider's nest.

And these children and their sons
At last rode through the cactus,
A cliff of mighty cowboys
On the lope,
With gun and rope.
And all the way to frightened Maine the old East heard them call,
And saw our Bryan by a mile lead the wall
Of men and whirling flowers and beasts,
The bard and the prophet of them all.
Prairie avenger, mountain lion,
Bryan, Bryan, Bryan, Bryan,
Gigantic troubadour, speaking like a siege gun,
Smashing Plymouth Rock with his boulders from the West,
And just a hundred miles behind, tornadoes piled across the sky,
Blotting out sun and moon,
A sign on high.

Headlong, dazed and blinking in the weird green light,
The scalawags made moan,
Afraid to fight.

II

When Bryan came to Springfield, and Altgeld gave him greeting,
Rochester was deserted, Divernon was deserted,
Mechanicsburg, Riverton, Chickenbristle, Cotton Hill,
Empty: for all Sangamon drove to the meeting—
In silver-decked racing cart,
Buggy, buckboard, carryall,
Carriage, phaeton, whatever would haul,
And silver-decked farm-wagons gritted, banged and rolled,
With the new tale of Bryan by the iron ties told.

The State House loomed afar.
A speck, a hive, a football,
A captive balloon—
And the town was all one spreading wing of bunting, plumes, and
                                        sunshine,
Every rag and flag, and Bryan picture sold,
When the rigs in many a dusty line
Jammed our streets at noon,
And joined the wild parade against the power of gold.

We roamed, we boys from High School,
With mankind,
While Sprinfield gleamed,
Silk-lined.
Oh, Tom Dines, and Art Fitzgerald,
And the gangs that they could get!
I can hear they yelling yet.
Helping the incantation,
Defying aristocracy,
With every bridle gone,
Ridding the world of the low down mean,
Bidding the eagles of the West fly on,
Bidding the eagles of the West fly on,
We were bully, wild and woolly,
Never yet curried below the knees.
We saw flowers in the air,
Fair as the Pleiades, bright as Orion,

—Hopes of all kind,
Made rare, resistless, thrice refined.
Oh, we bucks from every Springfield ward!
Colts of democracy—
Yet time-winds out of Chaos from the star-fields of the Lord.

The long parade rolled on. I stood by my best girl.
She was a cool young citizen, with wise and laughing eyes.
With my necktie by my ear, I was stepping on my dear,
But she kept like a pattern, without a shaken curl.

She wore in her hair a brave prairie rose.
Her gold chums cut her, for that was not the pose.
No Gibson Girl would wear it in that fresh way.
But we were fairy Democrats, and this was our day.

The earth rocked like the ocean, the sidewalk was a deck.
The houses for the moment were lost in the wide wreck.
And the bands played strange and stranger music as they trailed along.
Against the ways of Tubal Cain,
Ah, sharp was their song!
The demons in the bricks, the demons in the grass,
The demons in the bank-vaults peered out to see us pass,
And the angels in the trees, the angels in the grass,
The angels in the flags, peered out to see us pass.
And the sidewalk was our chariot, and the flowers bloomed higher,
And the street turned to silver and the grass turned to fire,
And then it was but grass, and the town was there again,
A place for women and men.

III

Then we stood where we could see
Every band,
And the speaker's stand
And Bryan took the platform.
And he was introduced.
And he lifted his hand
And cast a new spell.
Progressive silence fell
In Springfield,
In Illinois
Around the world,

Then we heard these glacial boulders across the prairie rolled:
"The People have a right to make their own mistakes. . . .
You shall not crucify mankind
Upon a cross of gold."

And everybody heard him —
In the streets and State House yard.
And everybody heard him
In Springfield,
In Illinois,
Around and around and around the world,
That danced upon its axis
And like a darling broncho whirled.

IV

July, August, suspense.
Wall Street lost to sense.
August, September, October,
More suspense,
And the whole East down like a wind-smashed fence.

Then Hanna to the rescue,
Hanna of Ohio
Rallying the roller-tops,
Rallying the bucket-shops.
Threatening drouth and death,
Promising manna,
Rallying the trusts against the bawling flannelmouth;
Invading misers' cellars,
Tin-cans, socks
Melting down the rocks,
Pouring out the long green to a million workers,
Spondulix by the mountain-load, to stop each new tornado,
And beat the cheapskate, blatherskite,
Populistic, anarchistic,
Deacon—desperado.

V

Election night at midnight:
Boy Bryan's defeat.
Defeat of western silver.

Defeat of the Wheat.
Victory of letterfiles
And plutocrats in miles
With dollar signs upon their coats,
Diamond watchchains on their vests
And spats on their feet.
Victory of custodians,
Plymouth Rock,
And all that inbred landlord stock.
Victory of the neat.
Defeat of the aspen groves of Colorado valleys,
The blue bells of the Rockies,
And blue bonnets of old Texas,
By the Pittsburg alleys.
Defeat of alfalfa and the Mariposa lily.
Defeat of the Pacific and the long Mississippi.
Defeat of the young by the old and silly.
Defeat of tornadoes by the poison vats supreme.
Defeat of my boyhood, defeat of my dream.

VI

Where is McKinley, that respectable McKinley,
The man without an angle or a tangle,
Who soothed down the city man and soothed down the farmer,
The German, The Irish, the Southerner, the Northerner,
Who climbed every greasy pole, and slipped through every crack;
Who soothed down the gambling hall, the bar-room, the church,
The devil vote, the angel vote, the neutral vote,
The desperately wicked, and their victims on the rack,
The gold vote, the silver vote, the brass vote, the lead vote,
Every vote? . . .

Where is McKinley, Mark Hanna's McKinley,
His slave, his echo, his suit of clothes?
Gone to join the shadows, with the pomps of that time,
And the flame of that summer's prairie rose.
Where is Cleveland whom the Democratic platform
Read from the party in a glorious hour,
Gone to join the shadows with pitchfork Tillman,
And sledge-hammer Altgeld who wrecked his power.

Where is Hanna, bulldog Hanna.
Low-browed Hanna, who said: "Stand pat"?
Gone to his place with old Pierpont Morgan.
Gone somewhere . . . with lean rat Platt.

Where is Roosevelt, the young dude cowboy,
Who hated Bryan, then aped his way?
Gone to join the shadows with mighty Cromwell
And tall King Saul, till the Judgment day.

Where is Altgeld, brave as the truth,
Whose name the few still say with tears?
Gone to join the ironies with Old John Brown,
Whose fame rings loud for a thousand years.

Where is that boy, that Heaven-born Bryan,
That Homer Bryan, who sang from the West?
Gone to join the shadows with Altgeld the Eagle,
Where the kings and the slaves and the troubadours rest.

The Eagle That Is Forgotten

(*John P. Altgeld. Born December 30, 1847; died March 12, 1902*)

Sleep softly . . . eagle forgotten . . . under the stone.
Time has its way with you there, and the clay has its own.
"We have buried him now," thought your foes, and in secret rejoiced.
They made a brave show of their mourning, their hatred unvoiced.
They had snarled at you, barked at you, foamed at you day after day.
Now you were ended. They praised you, . . . and laid you away.

The others that mourned you in silence and terror and truth,
The widow bereft of her crust, and the boy without youth,
The mocked and the scorned and the wounded, the lame and the poor
That should have remembered forever, . . . remember no more.

Where are those lovers of yours, on what name do they call
The lost, that in armies wept over your funeral pall?
They call on the names of hundred high-valiant ones,
A hundred white eagles have risen the sons of your sons,
The zeal in their wings is a zeal that your dreaming began
The valor that wore out your soul in the service of man.

Sleep softly, . . . eagle forgotten, . . . under the stone,
Time has its way with you there and the clay has its own.
Sleep on, O brave-hearted, O wise man, that kindled the flame—
To live in mankind is far more than to live in a name,
To live in mankind, far, far more . . . than to live in a name.

The Flower-Fed Buffaloes *

The flower-fed buffaloes of the spring
In the days of long ago,
Ranged where the locomotives sing
And the prairie flowers lie low;
The tossing, blooming, perfumed grass
Is swept away by wheat,
Wheels and wheels and wheels spin by
In the spring that still is sweet.
But the flower-fed buffaloes of the spring
Left us long ago.
They gore no more, they bellow no more,
They trundle around the hills no more: —
With the Blackfeet lying low,
With the Pawnees lying low.

   * from *Going-To-The-Stars* (1926).

The New Eden *

The wise and lovely serpent in the garden
Where our first parents lived in innocence
Offered them unknown fruit, and there commence
The fever known as sin, the dream called pardon.
To-day a sturdier Eve confronts the warden
Of the forbidden tree. She circumvents
Adam's hunger for sin with common sense;
Fed on wild crab-apples, their spirits harden.
Cynical innocents, they cling together,
It is a no-man's-land they wander in,
An uninspiring desert, flat and waste.
The older generation wonders whether
That fruit was really bitter to the taste,
Which opened to them the third dimension, sin.

Dingy Street

It is twilight at the dreary edge of town
And the December air
Is harsh and bitter. All the trees are bare,
The leaves are scattered and trodden down
To pulp, and every house is brown,
There is no trace of beauty anywhere.

Night comes slowly. The houses hide in the gloom,
But toward the muddy street
One by one their shabby windows bloom
Like golden flowers, to shine and greet
The bundled effigies on sodden feet
Trudging toward welcome in the hidden room.

There is a magic in it. There once more,
Body and spirit, they are warmed and fed;

* This and the following poems are from *The King With Three Faces and Other Poems* (1929).

There, as a thousand times before,
The ancient feast is spread,
The simple miracles of love and bread. . . .
They stumble into beauty at the door.

Pride

A flood of workmen surges up the hill
That rises heavy with welcome beneath their feet.
Earth hunches a shoulder under the paven street,
Feeling their footsteps, knowing her children still.

They swing their rugged bodies, proud to endure
A heavy day. They are able to forget
Their labor. Shaping iron they have sweat,
And forging steel, grown powerful and sure.

I think that Adam, after he passed outside
Eden, and by his own salt sweat had earned
His bitter bread, would never have returned
Once he had known the savor of such pride!

The Shop

The shop is black and crimson. Under the forge
Men hold red bars of iron with black iron tongs;
It crashes, sparks spatter out. It crashes again, again.
At last the iron is bent as it belongs.

Swedes, Norwegians, Poles, and Greeks, they are men;
They laugh when they please, look ugly when they please,
They wear black oakum in their ears for the noise,
They know their job, handle their tools with ease.

Their eyes are clean and white in their black faces;
If they like, they are surly, can speak an ugly *no;*
They laugh great blocks of mirth; their jokes are simple;
They know where they stand, which way they go.

If I wore overalls, lost my disguise
Of womanhood and youth, they would call me friend,
They would see I am one of them, and we could talk
And laugh together, and smoke at the day's end.

Youth Visits our Inferno

They call this hell! With deep disapprobation
For all of us, honest sinner and lusty saint,
Our visitors find us mildewed by the taint
Of old commandments. Their new dispensation
Has come too late for us and our salvation.
They find us pitiful and rather quaint
In our inferno. I make no complaint,
I am happier here with all my generation.
We are damned with the knowledge of good and evil: they
Whose new estate is freedom, suffer worse
And find life empty, trivial and boring,
A sort of game that every one must play,
And no one knows the rules, and no one's scoring,
And nothing's at stake, for youth has lost its purse.

Rain-Night *

The dogged rain
Of unawakened growths
Is hurling down its spear-points
Into our walks and streets.

*What new beauty
Are you striking out of dingy things?*

The little pawn-shop
Droops to the pavement
Battered and damp,
Its blue-lighted window
Guarding a stingy handful
Of cheap carved brass trays
Bird feathers, glass clocks,
And green candle-sticks.

People step tightly by
Dodging hither and thither
In the misty way.

But I have looked down into
These rain-spear-stung streets
And found mirrored there
An unguessed beauty of dingy things:

> Poured gold,
> Melted blue,
> Odd-shaped shadows of men.

Oh, I do not want realities!
Give me their misshapen lovely images
And unreached forms.

* This and the two poems following are from *The Living Frieze* (1921).

Mellow

These soft hours,
The color of blurred pebbles
And wan sand,
Are an old worn fringe
About the breasts
Of the mellow afternoon.

The lilac lake
Is a saucer—thin—
Burdened with faint blue rings.

The brown velvet dog
Is a curved attitude
Upon the lawn.

Jagged in the black tree-**lines**
The frayed sun languishes—
A plae pink poppy
Grown too large.

Chicago

O city of beauty,
They have spoken without understanding;
They have called you evil!

O city of beauty,
Maybe it is only my heart you have shaken
With your sadness of rose evenings,
And the shadows falling
In the misty evening
Under the bridges.

Your avenues are velvet and symmetrical,
As speech slow-moving

O city of Beauty,
I come not with vain enumeration!

For in the untrod night
I have looked upon your rapt
Presence.

There was a whiteness
                    as of wings stirring.

From "Memoria Technica" *

NIGHT LIGHTS

In the age of light
Even the night is full of light vibrations.
The observer looks upon no theatre,
And no re-creative reader reads a fantastic book:
Only a man with normal eyes
Sits in a brand new skyscraper
And looks out the windows
Which face the spaces that once were night.
He sees the indefatigable vibrations of light
Reeling and flooding over neighbor skyscrapers,
Over stone and steel bridges, over pavements,
And over the green river quivering
Hurling back the vibrations up-side-down.

From "Ensemble"

ON A DUNE

The point of view
From the ground
Made pale, slim grass
Shoot up as trees,
And the sparkling sea
Tend toward sky.

Out of fear,
Out of a man's dream,
Lay a snake
In the sand;

* from *A Marriage With Space* (1927), as are the succeeding poems by
Turbyfill.

But on request
It crawled away.

Hawks discoursed,
A cricket sang,
And leisurely and suave
A grasshopper slid
Down a swaying stem.

A warm, placid smell
Of sun and sweet marsh-grass
Rose up
And was hurled beyond
By a clear bright breeze
From the stirring sky-slanting sea.

From "Movies of Forgotten Emotion"

REALISTS
Hid under a bushel of rubbish
A poem exists—
Organized, effulgent.
They might dig up the vision,
But they keep throwing on another spade-ful:
"You don't know reality, haven't lived," they pile on.

"Living," they sleep the winter on a cross.
(Unseen uprights rise,
Beams of the poem structure organize.)
They hear steps on creaking stairs,
Hands scratching on a door,
And a voice that cries, "He's dead!"
(Descend to foundations
To learn the whereabouts of domes.)

They hire halls with borrowed money
And black their faces
For managers that don't come.
Under the cork white dreams despair,
But they sing funny songs about "weepin'."
They steal a fire-bucket's water
To absolve their eclipsed identity;

Then go sing Korosokow's songs
To a hungry gramophone—
Signing a colored prima donna's name.
(Houses of many mansions
Bought with neither money nor price
Echo with glad noises to a new-found name.)

"You don't know reality," they pile on.

Lost City *

We shall build it again though it caves in,
And the ramparts fall where the moss is,
And the draw-bridge no horseman crosses
Lets the dusk and the wind and the waves in.

We shall build it with hills and with hollows,
And small slopes where vineyards are sprawling,
And a wall that crumbles in falling,
And a river nobody follows.

Through the gateways we'll see to the center
Where fountains are playing, and flowers
Run a flame up the twilit towers
Of the city we never shall enter.

And the wind will die down in the streamers,
And the spires will fall with the nightfall;
But a door will open—a light fall
On a street that is peopled with dreamers.

Torch-Bearers

The women on the streets
With pretty faces and empty hearts,
Pretty homes and no love in them—
Torch-bearers wanting a flame!
Is there no Mecca for the pretty faces?—
No fetish for the tapering hands?
Is there no prophet big enough?
The pretty faces,
How they would shine
On a dark night
In single file!

* This and the following poems are from *The Lost City—Poems* (1928).

Hands holding candles,
White profiles moving slowly across the blackness —
Pretty women,
Torch-bearers,
With eyes lifted!

Fall of Snow

This, then, is wisdom. Watch with me the drifting
Of snow. Beyond the window see the street
White as a lily lifting
The noiseless imprint of feet.

Say with me: 'We are brave, we could mingle out
There with the crowd. We could blow with the snow.
But is it not wisdom to single out
This window and look below?'

'Is it not wisdom, in winter, to spare me
The desolate means with which we entice
Our love to bloom and to tear me
With a fragile flowering of ice?'

Stand at a window and hear the wind crying.
Let love be lost as the city is lost:
Over the eaves the snow flying;
And over the snow, the frost.

Will not the impartial sun when it lingers
And wavers like flame through the ice on the sill
Kindle our desolate fingers? . . .
Wiser to think that it will.

Excursion

Is it that forests have tree-trunks that streak their
Colors of charcoal into the ground?
Is it the color of leaves or the sound
That we seek there?

We who are part of the city, what makes us
Dare the enchantment of trees and the spaces
Where light is a dream on our upturned faces
And no sun wakes us?

What have we taken, as fragile as glass is,
Out of the forests where we have lain
And watched the light slide from the leaves like rain
When day passes?

And what do we ever recall of our searches?
Even to-day when the forest was brighter
We moved through the trees and our arms were whiter
Than all the birches.

Yet out of that green confusion of growing
We have returned to the city content—
These rooms we share are like trees that are bent
With their leaves blowing.

Bridges

Founding a constant grandeur
On inconstant sand,
Bridges hurdle rivers
And land.

Surly, their perfect sinews
Under long duress,
Holding a crouching posture
Motionless.

Beams arch high, and girders—
The Z-bar, the truss—
That we may cross laughing,
Oblivious.

That there is a river
Blackened by the night,
Where a mighty shadow
Glistens white.

Afternoon *

I came to an orchard—blossoms blowing
On twisted branches, trees inclined
By wind, all lunging west and throwing
Their shadows parallel behind.

A frail green wave of rain swept in
Flashing the sun like broken glass;
It threaded slanting through the thin
Black boughs; I stayed to see it pass.

It hurried out across the meadows
And in a wide bright mist was gone.
I stayed to watch the orchard shadows
Crawl east an inch, then wandered on;

But very soon I heard a mutter
Along the dusty road afresh,
And when I reached the pond the water
Was silver rings in a windy mesh.

Pantomime for a Spring Twilight

Dumb and vaguely to the vision
Like a ghost or apparition
Or a memory or dream,
Geese shall go in a pale stream
Through the blue misty air
Down a purple pathway where
Slender tall trees rise like smoke,
Black and wavering—with one oak
Near the bottom of the hill
In whose night shall wait a still
Patient boy, watching the broad
Pale birds lunging down the road

* This and the four poems following are from *Boy in the Wind* (1927).

Lightly: he shall watch and wait
Till a figure follow straight
Hard behind the glimmering geese,
Paler and more swift than these.

Twilight in a Tower

Finding the city below me like a flame
In the last sunshine, I said to autumn, "Blow on!
We are building a beautiful spring you cannot claim
In this country of stone."

And seeing so many men march in a thousand ways
The old way of hunger and thirst, I thought,
They are going somewhere, somewhere their dream is waiting,
Whether they know it or not.

But night came, smelling of far fields, and even
That brave procession moving with purpose and pride
Became like shadows wandering or driven,
And the wind cried,

And the world seemed a world of autumn and wind,
And the city but a frail rustling by the sea
Of men like leaves blown blindly without end
From life's wild flowering tree.

Fall of Stars

The snow came down like stars tonight
Over the city silently.
The air, like a great, glittering tree
Bloomed noiselessly with light.

I thought, it is the snow I see
Like stars. And it was long ago
That ever I saw the stars like snow.

And I thought of a boy, a long time dead,
Who dreamed such beauty out of pain
That music moved within his brain,
And the stars stormed about his head.

His ghost is like the wind, I said,
That cries into the crystal gloom
And wanders where the white clouds blow.

And I shall hear his song, I know,
Wherever the boughs of silence bloom
With snow like stars or stars like snow.

City of Wind

You ask, "Who is it you kiss when you kiss that way?"
You ask, "Where have your lips flown now?" And I, dissembling,
Protest. And what would you say if I should say,
"To a city of wind, a city of towers trembling?"

I thought I should tell how I wooed you for her sake,
Since she would not listen. But how could you understand—
You to whom love is a voice, a footstep, a hand—
What do you know of love that is only an ache?

What do you know of love that is only a want
At night in the wind, when even the buildings blow
And cry in their joists, and people are blown aslant
With fences and trees and the dumb drift of snow?

How can you understand that whatever I thirst for
It is nothing but shadows I am seeking,
Remembering a city at dusk and the wind speaking,
Remembering it was a dream that I longed first for?

And would you believe it is to a city of wind blowing
My heart must go home at last, a lover and child,
To lose its pain in her heart wholly, knowing
It is a heart of wind, hollow and wild?

The Dead Elm on the Hilltop *

This tree was burned by lightning to its root
In an October tempest many years ago now.
I can remember the lovely range of its bough,
Its scattered fruit,

---

* This and the remaining poems by Dillon are from *The Flowering Stone*
(1931).

Its voice as of waters on an invisible shore,
And the veined leaves transparent against the sky:
And so I have thought this tree could not die till I die.
Yet April comes no more

In a tall cloud of bronze to the top of the hill,
And summer stands no more in singing green.
And autumn, returning like a murderer to the scene,
Finds nothing left to kill.

September Moon

Above the continent I saw appear
For the last time in the last warmth of the year
The gibbous moon. I thought: It comes to shed
A last kind beam to kiss and loiter by
On all things derelict or left to die,
Being itself a thing abandoned and dead.
Now let all creatures hounded out of doors,
Love's waifs and felons whom the world abhors,
Make holiday until the cold rains start.
This moon goes with them even as my heart.

And when it laid my shadow at my feet
I thought of all things infamous and sweet,
All wayward craft whereon the moon is bright:
Of poor consanguines helplessly possessed
In the tall glittering cornfields of the west—
Of girl and girl in the New England night
For whom dead Lesbos lives—of boy and boy
Somehow surviving Crete in Illinois—
Of ladies and their lovers mouth to mouth
Deep in the south.

The Hours of the Day

The city stirred about me softly and distant.
Its iron voice flew upward into the air.
All day I wondered that I walked and listened
As if in freedom there—

And wondered how love so led me and removed me:
My breath coming deep and glad, for she had drawn it;
My eyes being wild with pride because she loved me;
My heart being shielded with her beauty upon it.

This Dream is Strange

This dream is strange that has not flown
Though summer from the sky has strewn
Her lovely laces on the dust:
This honeysuckle-scent not lost
With all the rain has washed away;
This verdure not exchanged for hay
And bundled up and borne to stall;
This bough most profitless of all,
But freighted with the pain of spring
Unfruitfully—the only thing
In forest, flower-bed, or field,
That still must bloom and may not yield.
Alas! far happier the bare
And dreamless orchard hung with air,
The meadow of its beauty mown,
The garden by the wind brought down
Whereon the sorrowful years depart—
And happier the broken heart,
Whose grieving is a wind gone by.
This love is strange that does not die.

The Summery Night Before The Frost

The summery night before the frost
My heart divined the frost was toward.
I saw the lake's wide iris lost
And the red flag of sunset lowered.

I thought: Farewell, remembered things!
These are the nights for nerveless sleeping.
Not music with her bells and strings
Could stir me into passion and weeping.

Such quiet ruin is in my breast,
Such peace upon my body has stolen,
I shall have drowned in dreamless rest
Love's memory ere the leaves are fallen.

Wherefore I came into the wood,
For there they fell past knowing or number,
And flung myself in solitude
Among their mindlessness to slumber.

But sleep for once was not my friend
By whom all creatures are befriended.
I wakened in the autumn wind
Hot with the dream that has not ended.

Cutting Weeds *

When he was twelve years old he cut the weeds
Along the fence where the cornfields swayed
In hot, slow-moving winds and, working, played
His scythe was turned a sword for mighty deeds.
He felt the might of conflict; met his needs
For great adventures with the thoughts that strayed
Like pageants through his mind, and he was made
The hero loved of ladies, knights, and steeds.

What ill winds blew that mist of dreams away? . . .
Grown into manhood now he swings his blade
With dogged, steady strokes along the fence.
He thinks, perhaps, of gold the corn will pay—
Is restless, vaguely troubled, half afraid
Of wishes haunting him with imminence.

Deserted Farms

About deserted farms there is a sense
Of waiting for the ones who went away.
Old orchards cling to fruit and by each fence
The morning-glory faces greet the day.
Through trees at twilight by each lane or wall,
Expectant whispers quicken when once more
Old doors may creak—in wind—and mow and stall
Awake to gusty feet along the floor.

The moon, from empty pastures on the hill,
At first seems like a lantern coming home,
And crickets, chirping far away and shrill,
Make sounds like laden axles over loam
The land stores richness waiting, and who knows
That waiting is in vain while longing grows!

* This and the three poems following are from *Selected Poems* (1931).

To Wild Geese over a Great City

Dark streams of pavements under misted light
    Flow endlessly by sheer walls groping high
And over muffled thunders of this night
    I hear again your mournful, cadenced cry.
I cannot see your dark wedge driving north
    Through slow rain but I know it wavers here
Above this sea of strange lights blinking forth
    To blind you if perchance you come too near . . .
Fly not too low this night lest you shall be
Frail wreckage tossed on this unheeding sea.

Through first chaff swirled from Winter's threshing floor,
    Past lonely fields and cliffs, I saw you go
To bask on sandbars of the south once more,
    And when I felt again the soft winds blow
A faint perfume of earth I knew that soon
    Would come your call across uncharted air
And I might see you pass before the moon . . .
    But on this night I hear you passing where
The moon is lost, and something lost in me
Cries back to you, above this glaring sea.

Man's inner blindness cries for outer light;
    Against the secret tide whose undertow
Pulls at him here this gesture of his might
    Wings up in stone; the purrs of dynamo
And motor, in his hours of darkness, keep
    His world in rhythm, and your wings must beat
Unknown across this night, above his sleep,
    Or fall a bloody offering at feet
Of some stone idol flashing sleepless eyes . . .
Your call fades northward on the misted skies.

Below you wild dreams blinded by the glare
    Have lost the way. Once they had followed you
To find new wonder waiting everywhere,
    Plains stretched to heights and waters to the blue . . .
Where muscles strain no longer, nerves are strained,
    Taut as the city's hidden net of wires.

What have we lost that all we here have gained
    Must leave us puzzled, thwarted by desires?
While one stands in this night to hear you go . . .
Not happier now . . . not more contented so.

A City Bridge in Snow

The lift of gray walls and a droop of gray
Sky like the weary wings of some lost gull
That, down these city canyons, took its way.
But suddenly this dawn is beautiful.
A jeweled arch, pure in smoke-laden airs,
A fantasy's design, a thing of wonder,
A span of utter loveliness, now bears
The dark stream over it, the gray stream under.

No architect had seen the patterned steel
Take on such splendor and no longer be
The thing we knew . . . This bridge now seems to feel
The touch of hands from starred infinity—
The touch of those same hands that have their way
Of mixing star-dust with the mortal clay!

Boy in a Coal Car *

Out of the smoke-blue field of timothy
I came to the railroad track with its hard brightness
Diminishing on the upward grade and ending
In smoky hazes to the west. A freight
Passed, heading west, and head and shoulders above
The edge of a coal car, I saw him watching me.
He was young and bareheaded, his hair like ripe wheat blowing,
And I saw white teeth flash in a smile. He waved.
He was on his way. . . . Two hundred years ago
A head like that might have been at the prow of a ship,
Tingling with spray and the sea wind, facing the world.
One hundred years ago a head like that
Might have faced the west from the seat of a covered wagon.
And twenty-two years ago such a head might have lifted

* This and the poem following are from *The Collected Poems of Glenn Dresbach*
    (1950).

Out of a trench and shouted, "Come on, you fellows!
Do you want to live forever?"
                              The freight rolled by
In a cloud of dust and I thought of the whirled dust blowing
Into his face and his hair like ripened wheat. . . .
Only the dust we had trampled and wheels had ground
Blowing into his face as he turned to the west!
Perhaps he could see through it. He was on his way.
Just motion is better than standing still with a weight
Sagging the shoulders. His head was against the sky.
I waved to him—and the freight had thundered by.

A Lonely Field

A lonely field soon gets in trouble.
    The hawks hang over it.
Vines along a fence will double
    Their weight to cover it.
Out of corners will drift the thistle
    And up from the dark will grope
The brier and burr; where good crops were,
    The hazel and thorn will bristle
        And climb the sunny slope.

Whoever thinks he has tamed a little
    Space of earth, to leave it
Alone and safe, will find the brittle
    Sprouts and seeds will weave it
New patterns—while a wildness crouches
    In every shadow there.
His ruts soon fill, and colors spill,
    And weeds from their little pouches
        Toss chaos on the air.

Even if he is old and sleeping
    On a hill beyond the town,
The ivy will pull, with no one keeping
    Watch, the red rose down.
Roots will start the neat stone leaning,
    Vines will grope from no where,
And flowers like flame cover date and name
    With their own arrogant meaning—
        If no one remembers to go there.

Bogie *

The black rain settles in our empty block.
The drunken street-lamps leer with sidelong eyes,
Dim and unholy.
Old newspapers grown restless in the gutter
With flap and flutter
Rise and subside and rise
It is half-past-twelve-o'clock
The night-goes-slowly.

I am awake again. I cannot sleep.
I light the lamp again and draw the shutter.
I light the lamp against the steps that creep
The sounds that mutter.
I draw the shutter against the lids that peep.

Something goes crouching at the dripping flank
Of the broken wall! Something in tatters slips
Down alleys dank!
Something from door to door before the rain
Dodges and whines. Something with twisting lips
Terribly smiles outside my shuttered pane.

Spring Comes to Chicago

My heart has told me, breathing low
How sunlit pastures after rain
Comb out their silken slopes again,
How marshland haunts we used to know
Are purple where the violets grow.

My traitor heart too well has told
How in a garden that we knew
The last pink crocus spills its dew,

* This and the two following poems are from *A Prayer Rug* (1923).

How sweet the hyacinths unfold
And how the jonquils preen their gold.

My heart has gone on homing feet
To seek Wisconsin fields again
Where robins steal the sprouting grain,
Forgetting that it once held sweet
This dingy wall and barren street

Oh chill gray city by the lake,
Where now the cold gulls scream and soar
And sullen waves against the shore
Sullenly rise and loudly break,
Much have I lost for your dear sake!

Midway Sketches

I

Along the Midway, hand in hand with me
New Winter walks.
Sweeter than rainy April is her breath,
Promise of colder days when bleaker trees,
Chiselled on copper skies
Will point their parable.
Delicately upon the fragile grass,
Constrained, with level brows,
Now on the Midway, hand in hand with me
New Winter walks.

II

Consort of Gea, primal, enigmatic,
Time stands above his pool,
While all the dark and pitiable tide
Of human life goes by.
Pulseless, not to be moved by prayer,
He stands.
A storm blows in out of the ancient lake,
And endlessly,
Down Cottage Grove, the rattling traffic runs.

III

Voices in darkness, footsteps on wet streets,
Pass and repass,
Hauntingly, irrevocably,
Into the velvet nap of night.
Why did you seek me, friends that I cannot see,
Faces I never know?

IV

And look where Harper with horned towers,
Encloses in its rugged Gothic skull,
The swarming, the incredible,
The many-faceted, the gamut-ranging,
The Student Brain.

A Convent Walk *

In green seclusion and unwavering light,
In larkspur-haunted leisure and dim peace
They mount the blue crescendo of July.
Between these walls the gay, abandoned world
Slips its impassioned pansies. Here the bold
Perfume of phlox is in the saintly air
And summer walks abroad.

Yet the nuns pace
Admirably along the walk
Beside the balsam bed,
Two and two, face and face,
Hands and hands,
Head and covered head,
Admirably they talk

. . . .

Why did I think too late
To compass my fragility with stone?

* from *The Long Leash* (1928).

The Mother *

She leans upon her window-sill to guess
Her children's passing in the summer night,
And feels their running feet and laughter press
Against her angled aureole of light.

Warm and invisible their presence seems
Tonight a fragile and imperiled spark,
And pitiful the hardihood that dreams
To quench with love this wide encroaching dark.

Out of the barley-field a rumor comes
Of grain immortal, and the pear-trees swell
With slow fruition, while the gourdlet drums
Heavy with seed beneath her window-sill.

And even now her murmuring body goes
Round the dark cycle with the ripening pod—
The bending barley and the bee-struck rose,
The apple fallen in the lap of God.

Dinner Party

The gentleman upon my right is prey
To some remote congenital distress.
It bites him when he wishes to be gay,
And makes a motley of his faultless dress.

Upon my left—phenomenon absurd—
I need be no psychiatrist to note
Beneath the wizened features of a bird
The jutting ego of a billy-goat

Why are we gathered in the twilight here?
Why do we graciously incline and speak?
(The lady with the diamond in her ear,
The lady with the wattle on her beak)

* This and the next three poems are from *Dinner Party* (1942).

And in what common secret are we wise?
Our eyes betray us. Look into the eyes.

Out of the wasted labor of the womb
And the worn night's indifference we came,
Each with his best defense against the gloom,
A cloak of velvet or a coat of fame.
Like ancient enemies we met at eight
With guarded sentences and looks withdrawn.
By half past nine our coffee and our hate,
Savored at leisure, were too quickly gone.

We rise and pace at leisure with our fears.
We find a common secret to disclose,
(The lady with the wattle on her ear,
The lady with the diamond in her nose.)
By half past ten we know ourselves to be
Foredoomed companions on a hostile sea.

Choreartium

No swan, no rose.
No posturing lover here, nor patterned sleep.
The bright air flows
Horizon-wide, sky-deep.
And girls with steadfast eyes
Rise from that light. Boys rise
Fearless as these.

They meet, They part. They meet.
They touch, but not for long.
The pure symphonic song
Informs their feet.
(Knowst thou the land?)
Here blows
The citrus-flower of peace.

The theatre is dark: outside we stand
Who lost too early and have found too late
That one-way-opening gate.

Apocalypse

Yea, verily, I saw
The rising sun, the hill,
The green world waking,
Trees shaking,
Hens scratching in the straw,
Sheep lying still.

At Bloomfield, Illinois,
This miracle befell.
(Attend me, choir of joy
Attest me, Gabriel!)
A barefoot boy
Drew water from a well.

I saw. And then flew wide
The barnyard gates and came
Men in blue raiment
To call the cows by name
And bid them come inside.

Yea, may I sicken
And may my tongue be stricken
If women did not go
Busily to and fro
With coffee and with bacon.

Thus saith the Lord:
My pasture still is sweet.
O angry men!
You who would beat
The plowshare to a sword
Turn back again.

At Bloomfield now
They plow.

Laughing Corn *

There was a high majestic fooling
Day before yesterday in the yellow corn.

And day after tomorrow in the yellow corn
There will be high majestic fooling.

The ears ripen in late summer
And come on with a conquering laughter,
Come on with a high and conquering laughter.

The long-tailed blackbirds are hoarse.
One of the smaller blackbirds chitters on a stalk
And a spot of red is on its shoulder
And I never heard its name in my life.

Some of the ears are bursting.
A white juice works inside.
Cornsilk creeps in the end and dangles in the wind.
Always—I never knew it any other way—
The wind and the corn talk things over together.
And the rain and the corn and the sun and the corn
Talk things over together.

Over the road is the farmhouse.
The siding is white and a green blind is slung loose.
It will not be fixed till the corn is husked.
The farmer and his wife talk things over together.

Crabapples

Sweeten these bitter wild crabapples, Illinois
October sun. The roots here came from the
wilderness, came before man came here. They
are bitter as the wild is bitter.

* This and the following poems are from *The Complete Poems of Carl Sandburg* (1950).

136

Give these crabapples your softening gold,
October sun, go through to the white wet
seeds inside and soften them black. Make
these bitter apples sweet. They want you, sun.

The drop and the fall, the drop and the fall,
the apples leaving the branches for the black
earth under, they know you from last year,
the year before last year, October sun.

The Letter S

The river is gold under a sunset of Illinois.
It is a molten gold someone pours and changes.
A woman mixing a wedding cake of butter and eggs
Knows what the sunset is pouring on the river here.
The river twists in a letter S.
     A gold S now speaks to the Illinois sky.

New Farm Tractor

Snub nose, the guts of twenty mules are in your cylinders and
     transmission.

The rear axles hold the kick of twenty Missouri jackasses.

It is in the records of the patent office and the ads there is twenty
     horsepower pull here.

The farm boy says hello to you instead of twenty mules—he sings to
     you instead of ten span of mules.

A bucket of oil and a can of grease is your hay and oats.

Rain proof and fool proof they stable you anywhere in the fields with
     the stars for a roof.

I carve a team of long ear mules on the steering wheel—it's good-by
     now to leather reins and the songs of the old mule skinners.

Joliet

On the one hand the steel works.
On the other hand the penitentiary.
Santa Fé trains and Alton trains
Between smokestacks on the west
And gray walls on the east.
And Lockport down the river.

Part of the valley is God's.
And part is man's.
The river course laid out
A thousand years ago.
The canals ten years back.

The sun on two canals and one river
Makes three stripes of silver
Or copper and gold
Or shattered sunflower leaves.
   Talons of an iceberg
   Scraped out this valley
   Claws of an avalanche loosed here.

Chicago

   Hog Butcher for the World,
   Tool Maker, Stacker of Wheat,
   Player with Railroads and the Nation's Freight Handler;
   Stormy, husky, brawling,
   City of the Big Shoulders:

They tell me you are wicked and I believe them, for I have seen your
   painted women under the gas lamps luring the farm boys.
And they tell me you are crooked and I answer: Yes, it is true I have
   seen the gunman kill and go free to kill again.
And they tell me you are brutal and my reply is: On the faces of
   women and children I have seen the marks of wanton hunger.
And having answered so I turn once more to those who sneer at this
   my city, and I give them back the sneer and say to them:
Come and show me another city with lifted head singing so proud to
   be alive and coarse and strong and cunning.

Flinging magnetic curses amid the toil of piling job on job, here is a
tall bold slugger set vivid against the little soft cities;
Fierce as a dog with a tongue lapping for action, cunning as a savage
pitted against the wilderness,
Bareheaded,
Shoveling,
Wrecking,
Planning,
Building, breaking, rebuilding,
Under the smoke, dust all over his mouth, laughing with white teeth,
Under the terrible burden of destiny laughing as a young man
laughs,
Laughing even as an ignorant fighter laughs who has never lost a
battle,
Bragging and laughing that under his wrist is the pulse, and under
his ribs the heart of the people,
Laughing!
Laughing the stormy, husky, brawling laughter of Youth, half-naked,
sweating, proud to be Hog Butcher, Tool Maker, Stacker of
Wheat, Player with Railroads and Freight Handler to the
Nation.

The Mayor of Gary

I asked the Mayor of Gary about the 12-hour day and the 7-day
week.
And the Mayor of Gary answered more workmen steal time on the
job in Gary than any other place in the United States.
"Go into the plants and you will see men sitting around doing
nothing—machinery does everything," said the Mayor of Gary
when I asked him about the 12-hour day and the 7-day week.
And he wore cool cream pants, the Mayor of Gary, and white shoes,
and a barber had fixed him up with a shampoo and a shave
and he was easy and imperturbable though the government
weather bureau thermometer said 96 and children were soaking
their heads at bubbling fountains on the street corners.
And I said good-by to the Mayor of Gary and I went out from the
city hall and turned the corner into Broadway.
And I saw workmen wearing leather shoes scruffed with fire and
cinders, and pitted with little holes from running molten steel,

And some had bunches of specialized muscles around their shoulder
 blades hard as pig iron, muscles of their forearms were sheet
 steel and they looked to me like men who had been some-
 where.

The Harbor

Passing through huddled and ugly walls
By doorways where women
Looked from their hunger-deep eyes,
Haunted with shadows of hunger-hands,
Out from the huddled and ugly walls,
I came sudden, at the city's edge,
On a blue burst of lake,
Long lake waves breaking under the sun
On a spray-flung curve of shore;
And a fluttering storm of gulls,
Masses of great gray wings
And flying white bellies
Veering and wheeling free in the open.

Washerwoman

The washerwoman is a member of the Salvation Army.
And over the tub of suds rubbing underwear clean
She sings that Jesus will wash her sins away
And the red wrongs she has done God and man
Shall be white as driven snow.
Rubbing underwear she sings of the Last Great Washday.

A Fence

Now the stone house on the lake front is finished and the workmen
 are beginning the fence.
The palings are made of iron bars with steel points that can stab the
 life out of any man who falls on them.
As a fence, it is a masterpiece, and will shut off the rabble and all
 vagabonds and hungry men and all wandering children look-
 ing for a place to play.
Passing through the bars and over the steel points will go nothing
 except Death and the Rain and Tomorrow.

Child of the Romans

The dago shovelman sits by the railroad track
Eating a noon meal of bread and bologna.
    A train whirls by, and men and women at tables
    Alive with red roses and yellow jonquils,
    Eat steaks running with brown gravy,
    Strawberries and cream, eclairs and coffee.
The dago shovelman finishes the dry bread and bologna,
Washes it down with a dipper from the water-boy,
And goes back to the second half of a ten-hour day's work
Keeping the road-bed so the roses and jonquils
Shake hardly at all in the cut glass vases
Standing slender on the tables in the dining cars.

From *The People, Yes* *

    The people, yes—
Born with bones and heart fused in deep and violent secrets
Mixed from a bowl of sky blue dreams and sea slime facts—
A seething of saints and sinners, toilers, loafers, oxen, apes
In a womb of superstition, faith, genius, crime, sacrifice—
The one and only source of armies, navies, work gangs,
The living flowing breath of the history of nations,
Of the little Family of Man hugging the little ball of Earth,
And a long hall of mirrors, straight, convex and concave,
Moving and endless with scrolls of the living,
Shimmering with phantoms flung from the past,
Shot over with lights of babies to come, not yet here.

    The honorable orators, the gazettes of thunder,
    The tycoons, big shots and dictators,
    Flicker in the mirrors a few moments
    And fade through the glass of death
    For discussion in an autocracy of worms
While the rootholds of the earth nourish the majestic people
And the new generations with names never heard of
Plow deep in broken drums and shoot craps for old crowns,
Shouting unimagined shibboleths and slogans,

* Included here are a part of Section 29 and all of Sections 57 and 107.

Tracing their heels in moth-eaten insignia of bawdy leaders —
Piling revolt on revolt across night valleys,
Letting loose insurrections, uprisings, strikes,
Marches, mass-meetings, banners, declared resolves,
Plodding in a somnambulism of fog and rain
Till a given moment exploded by long-prepared events —

.   .   .   .

Lincoln?
He was a mystery in smoke and flags
saying yes to the smoke, yes to the flags,
yes to the paradoxes of democracy,
yes to the hopes of government
of the people by the people for the people,
no to debauchery of the public mind,
no to personal malice nursed and fed,
yes to the Constitution when a help,
no to the Constitution when a hindrance,
yes to man as a struggler amid illusions,
each man fated to answer for himself:
Which of the faiths and illusions of mankind
must I choose for my own sustaining light
to bring me beyond the present wilderness?

Lincoln? was he a poet?
and did he write verses?
"I have not willingly planted a thorn in any man's bosom."
"I shall do nothing through malice; what I deal with is too vast for
    malice."

Death was in the air.
So was birth.
What was dying few could say.
What was being born none could know.

He took the wheel in a lashing roaring hurricane.
And by what compass did he steer the course of the ship?
"My policy is to have no policy," he said in the early months,
And three years later, "I have been controlled by events."
He could play with the wayward human mind, saying at Charleston,
    Illinois, September 18, 1858, it was no answer to an argument
    to call a man a liar.

"I assert that you [pointing a finger in the face of a man in the
    crowd] are here today, and you undertake to prove me a liar
    by showing that you were in Mattoon yesterday.
"I say that you took your hat off your head and you prove me a liar
    by putting it on your head."

He saw personal liberty across wide horizons.
"Our progress in degeneracy appears to me to be pretty rapid," he
    wrote Joshua F. Speed, August 24, 1855. "As a nation we
    began by declaring that 'all men are created equal, except
    negroes.' When the Know-Nothings get control, it will read 'all
    men are created equal except negroes and foreigners and
    Catholics.' When it comes to this, I shall prefer emigrating to
    some country where they make no pretense of loving liberty."

Did he look deep into a crazy pool
and see the strife and wrangling
with a clear eye, writing the military
head of a stormswept area:
"If both factions, or neither, shall abuse
you, you will probably be about right. Be
ware of being assailed by one and praised
by the other"?

Lincoln? was he a historian?
did he know mass chaos?
did he have an answer for those
who asked him to organize chaos?
"Actual war coming, blood grows hot, and blood is spilled. Thought
    is forced from old channels into confusion. Deception breeds
    and thrives. Confidence dies and universal suspicion reigns.
"Each man feels an impulse to kill his neighbor, lest he be first killed
    by him. Revenge and retaliation follow. And all this, as before
    said, may be among honest men only; but this is not all.
"Every foul bird comes abroad and every dirty reptile rises up. These
    add crime to confusion.
"Strong measures, deemed indispensable, but harsh at best, such men
    make worse by maladministration. Murders for old grudges,
    and murders for pelf, proceed under any cloak that will best
    cover for the occasion. These causes amply account for what
    has happened in Missouri."

Early in '64 the Committee of the New York Workingman's
   Democratic Republican Association called on him with assurances
   and he meditated aloud for them, recalling race and draft riots:
   "The most notable feature of a disturbance in your city last sum-
      mer was the hanging of some working people by other work-
      ing people. It should never be so.
   "The strongest bond of human sympathy, outside of the family
      relation, should be one uniting all working people, of all
      nations and tongues and kindreds.
   "Let not him who is houseless pull down the house of another,
      but let him labor diligently and build one for himself, thus by
      example assuring that his own shall be safe from violence
      when built."

   Lincoln? did he gather
   the feel of the American dream
   and see its kindred over the earth?

   "As labor is the common burden of our race,
   so the effort of some to shift
   their share of the burden
   onto the shoulders of others
   is the great durable curse of the race."

      "I hold,
   if the Almighty had ever made a set of men
   that should do all of the eating
   and none of the work,
   he would have made them
   with mouths only, and no hands;
   and if he had ever made another class,
   that he had intended should do all the work
   and none of the eating,
   he would have made them
   without mouths and all hands."
   "—the same spirit that says, 'You toil and
      work and earn bread, and I'll eat it.' No
      matter in what shape it comes, whether
      from the mouth of a king who seeks to
      bestride the people of his own nation
      and live by the fruit of their labor, or
      from one race of men as an apology for

enslaving another race, it is the same
tyrannical principle."

"As I would not be a *slave,* so I would not
be a *master.* This expresses my idea of
democracy. Whatever differs from this,
to the extent of the difference, is no
democracy."

"I never knew a man who wished to be himself
a slave. Consider if you know any
good thing that no man desires for himself."

"The sheep and the wolf
are not agreed upon a definition
of the word liberty."

"The whole people of this nation
will ever do well
if well done by."

"The plainest print cannot be read
through a gold eagle."

"How does it feel to be President?" an Illinois
friend asked.

"Well, I'm like the man they rode out of
town on a rail. He said if it wasn't for
the honor of it he would just as soon
walk."

Lincoln? he was a dreamer.
He saw ships at sea,
he saw himself living and dead
in dreams that came.

Into a secretary's diary December 23, 1863
went an entry: "The President tonight
had a dream. He was in a party of plain
people, and, as it became known who
he was, they began to comment on his
appearance. One of them said: 'He is a

very common-looking man.' The President
replied: 'The Lord prefers common-
looking people. That is the reason
he makes so many of them.' "

He spoke one verse for then and now:
   "If we could first know where we are,
   and whither we are tending,
   we could better judge
   what to do, and how to do it."

　.　.　.　.　.　.　.　.　.　.　.

      The people will live on.
The learning and blundering people will live on.
      They will be tricked and sold and again sold
And go back to the nourishing earth for rootholds
      The people so peculiar in renewal and comeback,
      You can't laugh off their capacity to take it.
The mammoth rests between his cyclonic dramas.

The people so often sleepy, weary, enigmatic,
is a vast huddle with many units saying:
   "I earn my living.
   I make enough to get by
   and it takes all my time.
   If I had more time
   I could do more for myself
   and maybe for others.
   I could read and study
   and talk things over
   and find out about things.
   It takes time.
   I wish I had the time."

The people is a tragic and comic two-face:
hero and hoodlum: phantom and gorilla twisting
to moan with a gargoyle mouth: "They
buy me and sell me . . . it's a game . . .
sometime I'll break loose . . ."

   Once having marched
   Over the margins of animal necessity,

Over the grim line of sheer subsistence
    Then man came
To the deeper rituals of his bones,
To the lights lighter than any bones,
To the time for thinking things over,
To the dance, the song, the story,
Or the hours given over to dreaming,
    Once having so marched.

Between the finite limitations of the five senses
and the endless yearnings of man for the beyond
the people hold to the humdrum bidding of work and food,
while reaching out when it comes their way
for lights beyond the prism of the five senses,
for keepsakes lasting beyond any hunger or death.
    This reaching is alive.
The panderers and liars have violated and smutted it.
    Yet this reaching is alive yet
    for lights and keepsakes.

    The people know the salt of the sea
    and the strength of the winds
    lashing the corners of the earth.
    The people take the earth
    as a tomb of rest and a cradle of hope.
    Who else speaks for the Family of Man?
    They are in tune and step
    with constellations of universal law.

    The people is a polychrome,
    a spectrum and a prism
    held in a moving monolith,
    a console organ of changing themes,
    a clavilux of color poems
    wherein the sea offers fog
    and the fog moves off in rain
    and the labrador sunset shortens
    to a nocturne of clear stars
    serene over the shot spray
    of northern lights.

    The steel mill sky is alive.
    The fire breaks white and zigzag

shot on a gun-metal gloaming.
Man is a long time coming.
Man will yet win.
Brother may yet line up with brother:

This old anvil laughs at many broken hammers.
There are men who can't be bought.
The fireborn are at home in fire
The stars make no noise.
You can't hinder the wind from blowing
Time is a great teacher
Who can live without hope?

In the darkness with a great bundle of grief
the people march.
In the night, and overhead a shovel of stars for
keeps, the people march:
"Where to? what next?"

Peace Between Wars

Between the long wars
there has always been peace
and likewise
between the short wars.

The longer the wars
the less was the peace
while the wars went on
and the shorter the wars
the sooner the peace came.

Whenever the peace
came to an end
the resulting war
always ran
either short or long.

Whenever a war ended
the resulting peace
ran till the next war.

Thus each peace
had its punctuation
by a war short or long
and each war at its end
ushered in an era
of peace short or long.

Therefore we know
absolutely,
incontestably,
the peace we now see
will run
till the next war begins
whereupon peace
will be ushered in
at the end of the next war.

Beyond this
we know little
absolutely, incontestably

A Million Young Workmen, 1915

A million young workmen straight and strong lay stiff on the grass
and roads,
And the million are now under soil and their rottening flesh will in
the years feed roots of blood-red roses.
Yes, this million of young workmen slaughtered one another and
never saw their red hands.
And oh, it would have been a great job of killing and a new and
beautiful thing under the sun if the million knew why they
hacked and tore each other to death.
The kings are grinning, the kaiser and the czar—they are alive riding
in leather-seated motor cars, and they have their women and
roses for ease, and they eat fresh poached eggs for
breakfast, new butter on toast, sitting in tall water-tight
houses reading the news of war.
I dreamed a million ghosts of the young workmen rose in their shirts
all soaked in crimson . . . and yelled:
God damn the grinning kings, God damn the kaiser and the czar.

The Long Shadow of Lincoln: *A Litany*

> (*We can succeed only by concert. . . . The dogmas of
> the quiet past are inadequate to the stormy present. The
> occasion is piled high with difficulty, and we must rise
> with the occasion. As our case is new so we must think
> anew and act anew. We must disenthrall ourselves. . . .
> December 1, 1862.* The President's Message to Congress.)

Be sad, be cool, be kind,
remembering those now dreamdust
hallowed in the ruts and gullies,
solemn bones under the smooth blue sea,
faces warblown in a falling rain.

Be a brother, if so can be,
to those beyond battle fatigue
each in his own corner of earth
    or forty fathoms undersea
    beyond all boom of guns,
    beyond any bong of a great bell,
    each with a bosom and number,
    each with a pack of secrets,
each with a personal dream and doorway
and over them now the long endless winds
    with the low healing song of time,
    the hush and sleep murmur of time.

Make your wit a guard and cover.
Sing low, sing high, sing wide.
Let your laughter come free
remembering looking toward peace:
"We must disenthrall ourselves."

Be a brother, if so can be,
to those thrown forward
for taking hardwon lines,
for holding hardwon points
    and their reward so-so,
little they care to talk about,
their pay held in a mute calm,

highspot memories going unspoken,
what they did being past words,
what they took being hardwon.
    Be sad, be kind, be cool.
        Weep if you must
    And weep open and shameless
        before these altars.

There are wounds past words.
There are cripples less broken
than many who walk whole.
    There are dead youths
    with wrists of silence
    who keep a vast music
    under their shut lips,
what they did being past words,
their dreams like their deaths
beyond any smooth and easy telling,
having given till no more to give.

    There is dust alive
with dreams of The Republic,
with dreams of the Family of Man
flung wide on a shrinking globe
    with old timetables,
    old maps, old guide-posts
    torn into shreds,
    shot into tatters,
    burnt in a firewind,
    lost in the shambles,
    faded in rubble and ashes

    There is dust alive
Out of a granite tomb,
Out of a bronze sarcophagus,
Loose from the stone and copper
Steps a whitesmoke ghost
Lifting an authoritative hand
In the name of dreams worth dying for,
In the name of men whose dust breathes
    of those dreams so worth dying for,
what they did being past words,
beyond all smooth and easy telling.

Be sad, be kind, be cool,
remembering, under God, a dreamdust
hallowed in the ruts and gullies,
solemn bones under the smooth blue sea,
faces warblown in a falling rain.

Sing low, sing high, sing wide.
Make your wit a guard and cover.
Let your laughter come free
like a help and a brace of comfort.

    The earth laughs, the sun laughs
over every wise harvest of man,
over man looking toward peace
by the light of the hard old teaching:
    "We must disenthrall ourselves."

Cool Tombs

When Abraham Lincoln was shoveled into the tombs, he forgot the
    copperheads and the assassin . . . in the dust, in the cool tombs.
And Ulysses Grant lost all thought of con men and Wall Street, cash
    and collateral turned ashes . . . in the dust, in the cool tombs.

Pocahontas' body, lovely as a poplar, sweet as a red haw in Novem-
    ber or a pawpaw in May, did she wonder? does she remember?
      . . . in the dust, in the cool tombs?

Take any streetful of people buying clothes and groceries, cheering a
    hero or throwing confetti and blowing tin horns . . . tell me if
      the lovers are losers . . . tell me if any get more than
      the lovers . . . in the dust . . . in the cool tombs.

From Exile *

Worn by the years two score in wars and wanderings,
Toils and joys, with many a lonely heartache
Such as men, wherever born, are heir to,
    Now as of olden;

Living in exile, loving Ronsard's roses,
Shakespeare's greenwood, Shelley's Tuscan skylark,
No whit less than the bobolinks and cornfields
    Near to my infancy;

Finding earth's face wild and beautiful everywhere,
Heartbeats passionate everywhere, all men piteous,
Turn I now, and nonetheless, to the prairie
    State that bore me.

Illinois, I come in love and lowliness.
Hither, where first I stared at the stars in wonderment,
Long my memories, long my homing thoughts have
    Lovingly tended.

Would I had known the buffalo herd in the grassland,
Lolled at night by the painted redskins' campfire,
Seen the French canoes, with priest and trader,
    Proffer the peace-pipe.

Indian trail and deerpath, hunter, settler,
These our prairie boys will brood on always,
Keeping with ardor of play that vanished wilderness
    Virgin eternally.

Here, a century gone, my father's grandfather,
Riding west from the banks of the clear Ohio,

---

* "From Exile" and the following poem, "Wherever Bees," are from *Poems Between Wars* (1941).

Hewed for a homestead logs of oak and butternut,
    Plowed the grassland.

Here, in a loamy stretch of corn and pumpkin,
Where by fence rail sunflowers grew, and hollyhock,
Laughed and sang my mother through a girlhood
    Sweet as the clover.

Born here, bred here, ten full years I dwelt here,
All in a small white cottage under a haw tree,
Dreamed old wars, played Indians, feared Jehovah,
    First saw elfland.

Here on my lips the wild bee dripped its honey,
Fireflies brushed my eyes with an eerie lantern,
Sun put passion, thunderstorms put mystery
    Into my heart pangs.

Illinois, O Illinois, your children,
Nurtured thus, though faring far and fearless
Endlessly over this earth, our spinning planet,
    Never forget you.

Let this sheaf of proud yet humble song, then,
Though but an hour, shine bright as a silver winter,
Green as May, glow red and gold as an autumn
    Day in boyhood.

Wherever Bees

(COMPIEGNE)

Wherever bees loot fields to fill a comb,
Or flowers in winds of waterfalls are fanned,
Or drowsy breakers on dove-breasted sand
Uncurl their deep-sea hues in creamy foam;
Wherever simple people plow the loam,
Living content and kind, as nature planned,
With brooks and cooling trees upon the land,
And fire for autumn nights, I am at home:
No less in the dews of these old French deer parks
Than picking black-eyed Susans out along

The country railroad, Sundays, as a boy;
Thrilled no less now to hear these April larks
In foreign sky, than, long ago, the song
Of April bobolinks, in Illinois.

Swarms *

Not death is conqueror,
But life, and always life.
Here on this weedy bank,
In lust of summer heat,
The quick fantastic host
Contend in fertile strife,
Divide and thrust and swell,
Beget and spawn and eat.

A bird unearths a worm,
A bee goes mumbling by,
The grasses tussle up
Or droop their heads in seed:
About a mouse's corpse,
The prey of pregnant fly,
The carrion beetles dig,
The ant battalions feed.

A milkweed sows its white
Balloons upon the breeze;
Two sweetheart butterflies
Across the road are blown;
Within the silky snare
The spider swings at ease;
The mosses' hidden claws
Attack the sleeping stone.

In rattling wagon pass
A rustic boy and girl;
His arm has won her waist,
A flush inflames her face,
And life will sweep them on

---

* "Swarms" and the following poem, "After Rain," are from *The Mothering Land: Selected Poems, 1918–1958* (1960).

With sure delirious whirl
Till passion has its way,
In the blood's distraught embrace.

I, too, am wide adrift:
With boasting and with song
I hide the dull suspense
That on my spirit weighs;
And when I make pretense
To stem that current strong,
With stern triumphant tide
It floats me down the days.

After Rain

After rain the air is cool, and clover-scented.
Peace has come to the mothering land; it has confessed
The season's pain to heaven, and been with pity blessed;
The blossoms wear a smile, the branches breathe contented,
Birds resume their song, and now, as breezes freshen,
The white and holy clouds depart in slow procession.

Midland *

Under the great cold lakes, under the midmost
Parallel that Lisbon too lies under—
Vesuvius and Corinth, Ararat,
Peking and Chosen, yellow and blue seas
Enormous, then the redwoods, then high Denver—
Under the wet midnorth, under cool Canada,
Swings my own West, directionless; the temperate,
The tacit, the untold. There was I born,
There fed upon the dish of dreaming land
That feeds upon itself, forever sunk
From the far rim, from crust and outer taste,
Forever lost and pleased, as circling currents
Swim to themselves, renumbering Sargasso
Centuries a wind brings round the world.
There am I still, if no thought can escape
To edges from that soft and moving center,
That home, that floating grave of what would fly
Yet did not: my own boyhood, meditating
Unto no end, eternal where I was.

The Cornetist

When the last freight, dusk-musical, had gone,
Groaning along the dark rails to St. Louis,
When the warm night, complete across the cornfields,
Said there was nothing now, no motion left,
No possible sound, we heard him:
Rocked on the silent porch and heard the low notes

Leave on their level errand like the last sound
Ever to be man-blown about the earth.
Like the last man this sentry of the switches

* This and the following poems are from *Collected and New Poems, 1924–1963*
  (1963).

Blew, and the mournful notes, transcending cinders,
Floated above the corn leaves:
Floated above the silks, until arriving,

Arriving, they invaded our warm darkness,
Deep in the still verandah, and we laughed:
"Why, there he is, that pitiful lone devil;
There is the Frisco nightingale again,
There is our mocking-bird-man" —
Laughed, and said these things, and went to bed.

And slept; but there are nights now when I waken,
After these years, and all these miles away,
When I sit up and listen for the last sound
Man will have made alive; and doubt a little
Whether we should have laughed;
Whether we should have pitied that poor soul.

You were too sure of being there forever,
And I too soon was leaving to be wise.
Not that his horn had wisdom; but at nighttime
Man has a need of man, and he was there,
Always; the horn was there
Always; and joy, I think, was why we laughed.

And slept; for there is many an hour of drearness,
Many an hour unloud with lips or brass,
When I lie still and listen for the last note
Ever some lung has blown; and am self-envious,
Thinking I once could laugh;
Thinking I once could pity that poor soul.

Family Prime

Our golden age was then, when lamp and rug
Were one and warm, were globe against the indifferent
Million of cold things a world contains.
None there. A light shone inward, shutting out
All that was not corn yellow and love young.

Like winter bears we moved, our minds, our bodies
Jointed to fit the roundness of a room:

As sluggish, and as graceful, whether couch
Or table intercepted, or if marbles
Clicked on the floor and hunched us into play.

How long? I do not know. Before, a blank.
And after, all this oldness, them and me,
With the wind slicing in from everywhere,
And figures growing small. I may remember
Only a month of this. Or a God's hour.

Yet I remember, and my father said
He did: the moment spherical, that age
Fixes and gilds; eternity one evening
Perfect, such as maybe my own sons,
And yours, will know the taste of in their time.

Going Home

His thought of it was like a button pressed.
Far away the figures started going;
A silver watch ticked in a sleepy vest,
And on the porch an apron string was blowing.

His thought again was like a fly-wheel cranked,
And circular machinery set gliding.
The little town turned truly, as the banked
Brown houses followed in and out of hiding.

His travel, once he went, was like the troop
Of farmers in an autumn to the fair.
All year the field was flat, but now the coop
Of turkeys and the horses would be there;

People moving everywhere and nodding,
Little boys with birds and yellow whips;
A person at a counter would be wadding
Rifles, and the girls would hold their hips.

His coming near was like the soft arrival
Of gods around a thing that they have made;
And will again forget; but long survival
Saves it, once again the trance is laid.

Bailey's Hands

The right one that he gave me —
I could have shut my eyes
And heard all seventy summers
Rasping at their scythes.

The left one that he lifted,
Tightening his hat —
I could have seen the cut groves
Lie fallen, green and flat;

Or seen a row of handles,
Ash-white and knuckle-worn,
Run back as far as boyhood
And the first field of thorn:

The two-edged axe and sickle,
The pick, the bar, the spade,
The adze, and the long shovel —
Their heads in order laid,

Extending many an autumn
And whitening into bone,
As if the past were marching,
Stone after stone.

So by his hands' old hardness,
And the slow way they waved,
I understood the story:
Snath-written, helve-engraved.

Defeated Farmer

Lift as he will a wordless face
To an earless wind, to a sightless sky,
He is not told if meadows lie
Beyond the rumor of the race
He ran and lost; and found disgrace
With common trees that standing die.

He can no more escape the scorn
Of day, that loathes a failing thing,
Than the stripped oak can beat a wing
And fly the wood where it was born;
Falling at night in a forlorn
Contrary wood where mold-worms sing.

Once he thought the wind conspired
With wet and dry and hot and cold
To slave for him. But he is old,
And long ago the year was tired,
And if the wind was ever hired
It bustled off to better gold.

Once he felt the city's eyes
In envy on him as he swung
Ill storms away. But not a tongue
Proclaims him lately weather-wise,
And he has heard towered laughter rise
From throats that in their turn are young.

He still can lift a lidded gaze
And count the mornings light and dark.
So the stripped elm with fallen bark
Receives the days. But not its days.
The greener wood has private ways
That posted death may not remark.

Culture of Corn

The great machines that mouse these fields
In May, between the long, dark showers—
How they do master and despise
The stick, the hoe that once were ours.

Even the coulter, tearing sod,
Even the horses, our huge slaves—
The red machines remember nothing.
Man and beast are in their graves,

And only metal that moves itself
Goes back and forth here, biting in.
Yet truth to say, the softened fields,
Supine, are willing that it win.

They lie there, those great breeding queens,
Brown at the breast and cool of womb,
And wait for seed; nor ever sigh
Because no two feet, four feet come.

Granary

The tall new crib is woven steel:
A humming cylinder in wind—
This wind—that once on weathered boards
Stopped dead. It made no music then,
Nor knows perhaps it whispers now
Among the meshes of such walls.

So high it is, so huge and old,
It may not hear what things it does,
It may not care if wood or wire,
If buildings, if October trees,
Stand out of earth a little way,
Opposing it a little while.

Come closer. Listen, and look up.
The whole sky—does it seem to sound?
But let your memory climb too,
And spread and spread till this be gone.
What did we say? Did something sing?
Does corn still blossom? Are there men?

The Only World

The meadow hedge hides meadowlarks
Whose voices rise as rise the roses,
Breaking at the top in bloom
Of sound and scent while daytime dozes;

Dozes over wind and dust;
Dozes over tractor roar—
Behemoth of the middle world
Murders music more and more.

Yet here by hedge the hidden throat,
The buried thorn decline the death;
Sending bubbles up and up
Of sweetly broken heart and breath

Till every leaf is overlaid,
Till every drop of air is drowned,
And sleepy daytime dreams again
Of its own scent, of its own sound.

This is the only world that was;
That will be when Behemoth dies;
That is at all, the meadowlarks
And roses murmur as they rise.

After Long Drought

After long drought, commotion in the sky;
After dead silence, thunder. Then it comes,
The rain. It slashes leaves, and doubly drums
On tin and shingle; beats and bends awry
The flower heads; puddles dust, and with a sigh
Like love sinks into grasses, where it hums
As bees did once, among chrysanthemums
And asters when the summer thought to die.

The whole world dreamed of this, and has it now.
Nor was the waking easy. The dull root
Is jealous of its death; the sleepy brow
Smiles in its slumber; and a heart can fear
The very flood it longed for, roaring near.
The spirit best remembers being mute.

4. SOME CONTEMPORARIES

EVEN WITHOUT the aid of an adequate historical perspective, some generalizations, albeit tentative ones, can be made concerning poetic activity in Illinois from 1940 to the present. This, however is not to suggest that in essence it is different from that in America generally in this period. The poetry by Illinois writers compared with that which we have sampled in the earlier periods is less Illinois in character, more revealing of the poet and less so of the place. Paradoxically, the poets seem less obviously subjective and comparatively more concerned with form, with the manner of their oblique revelations. These judgments are on the period taken as a whole and are partly in error if applied to every poetic creation, for there are real evidences of a recent shift to a more direct subjectivity.

Presumably the prime reason for a reduced sectionalism in Illinois poetry is the decline of sectionalism throughout the United States. An increased urbanization has led or is rapidly leading to a considerable national homogeneity. This development, with an accompanying human mobility—frequently made greater for the poet through his academic connections—has contributed to a greater concern with the personal situation in an impersonal culture and less with geographical connections. Thus, granted that the poem has always revealed subjective attitudes and feelings, a poem about Chicago today is likely to tell us less about a Chicago that we can see and recognize and more about the psyche, the heart of the poet. That this is often communicated by a relatively objective expression may be traceable to cultural influences such as the scientific and technical impersonality of contemporary life, not to mention a continuing symbolic reaction to earlier romantic subjectivities, though this reaction may in turn have been culturally determined. Also it is worth noting, without necessarily claiming an influence, that in reading the Illinois poets of these years one discovers various similarities to the art of Eliot and Cummings and, perhaps increasingly, to William Carlos Williams. Because these characteristics are present generally in contemporary poetry, the Illinois principle of selection has been somewhat less applicable in this section, though it has remained a helpful guide and has been used as far as possible.

In choosing the contemporary poets and poems, even more than in making the selections for the preceding periods, it has been necessary to be satisfied with a sampling. A vast amount of poetry by a great many Illinois poets has been produced in these years and is being written today. It is of such an extent that it is not possible in any reasonable time to locate and evaluate more than a representative part. I am quite certain, for example, that there are a number of effective poets writing as faculty members and as students in the various Illinois universities and colleges of whom I have not become aware; and the same is true of many other Illinois writers of poetry publishing in the multitude of little magazines in and out of the state. Given these limiting factors as well as that of space, the aim has been to select a fair number of poets of quality who are representative of most of the varying types of poetic activity in Illinois during the last twenty-five years or so, with a special concern to include some of the poets who are writing here at present. Again a few of the "borderline" poets, as they were labeled in the preceding section, have been omitted, among whom Karl Shapiro is no doubt the best known. Granted his Illinois association through the editorship of *Poetry* in the early fifties and his recent return to the University of Illinois at the Chicago Circle Campus, it remains true that in most persons' minds his major poetic connection is still with Nebraska.

Elder Olson, the first poet of this section, was born, educated, and has had, in the main, his professional life in Illinois, though this orientation has not set geographical or intellectual limits to his poetry. As Professor of English at the University of Chicago he is well known for his critical writings as well as for his poetry. Isabella Gardner (Mrs. Allen Tate) through most of her life and through most of her poetic activity has been of the Chicago area, and for some time in the 1950's was associate editor of *Poetry*. John Frederick Nims is at present Professor of English at the University of Illinois, Chicago Circle, having formerly taught at Urbana. He has had a varied geographical acquaintance in America and abroad, but basically it has been in the Midwest with a focus in Illinois since the

1940's. Gwendolyn Brooks, though originally from Kansas, has been a Chicago-based poet since fairly early in her career and among her other ways of speaking has been a Chicago-voiced poet. She received the Pulitzer Prize for poetry in 1950, and in 1968 was appointed Poet Laureate of Illinois following the death of Carl Sandburg. Henry Rago was born in Chicago and much—though not all—of his teaching and writing career has been in the Midwest, including years at Notre Dame, Depaul, and the University of Chicago. Since 1955, when he succeeded Karl Shapiro, he has been editor of *Poetry* and is now also at the University of Chicago as Professor of Literature and Theology, jointly in the New Collegiate Division and the Divinity School. In Lisel Mueller, a native of Germany, Illinois is fortunate in having a significant poet choose this state as her new home. Though her education and the character of her outlook has been shaped substantially by her American location, she has fruitfully retained something of a European perspective. Robert Sward is an "Illinois Poet" who is not at present writing here, but he is one with a strong Illinois experience—childhood in Chicago and education at the University of Illinois—which is revealed in a goodly number of his poems. Paul Carroll was born in Chicago, received his M.A. in English at the University of Chicago, and continued his Illinois connection as poetry editor of the *Chicago Review* and as founder and editor of *Big Table*. Recently he has been at the University of Iowa. Although Lucien Stryk, who grew up in Chicago, has had a varied study and teaching experience abroad, including Japan, his background is essentially midwestern—Iowa and Indiana in addition to Illinois. At present he teaches poetry, creative writing, and Oriental literature at Northern Illinois University. Just about all of R. R. Cuscaden's varied literary activity has been carried on in Illinois. Apart from his own poetry writing, this activity has been largely directed toward editing, ranging from editorial work with an industrial publication to the founding and editing of a number of little magazines, including the poetry magazine, *Midwest.*

Spring Ghost *

Just now, in snowy woods somewhere,
The first arbutus leaves break clear
Secretly, while yet the day
Lies an hour or so away,
And trees know. The barbed crystal star
Wanes westward, and at five there are
Lanterns borne slowly toward the shed
Amid the dark snows, and in bed
Wan sleepers sigh and turn: at six
A frosty light comes up and takes
The topmost vane above the barns,
And cattle stand with hay in horns
Beyond the luminous window-square
To watch the red round sun in air,
And harness reddens on the wall,
And rump by rump in the vague stall
Amid the glimmering straw the broad
Sleek stallion and his mare must stand,
And in the changing glow beyond,
The new colt, rusty-haired and rough,
Drinks burnished water from the trough,
And mice peep sharp-eyed out from straw.

By mid-morning the first thaw
Discovers leaves and fragile bones
Of field-mice, and bird-skeletons,
Draws from the charged earth the deep worm
That stony hail and winterstorm
Drove under; the prismatic air
Flows bright and chill as snow-water.
Blue as ice the puddles lie,
Reflecting cloud and branch and sky
And wings; and the slow spring at last
Builds up what autumn has laid waste.

* This and the following poems, unless otherwise indicated, are from *Collected Poems* (1963).

168

And he that walks, arisen again,
Shall find the iridescent thin
Corselet of the serpent's skin,
Cast when the pulsing snake no more
That diamond armour could endure,
And the curious winding-cloth
Wherein the worm became the moth;
But not in the scarce-flowering brake
Fallen, nor drowned in the pure lake,
Nor crumpled amid winter grass,
The dead youth that he once was.

For the Demolition of a Theater

The player was neither king nor clown;
Of tragedy or comedy,
Truth is the last catastrophe.

Paper castles, too, fall down;
Spider and mouse have always known
A false world ends in real debris.

This is the scene none cared to see,
True autumn in the plaster tree.
Walk the mouldering stage, alone,

Put on the dimmed and battered crown,
Mount the cobwebbed cardboard throne,
Command the ruinous painted sea;

O Prince of dreams, mock-Majesty,
Nothing stays the ruinous sea;
Even the painted waves roll on.

Even the dreamt kingdoms drown.

Jack-in-the-Box

Devil sprang from box,
Frightening the children, who would not be comforted.
In vain they were wooed with all the other toys;
Expecting new terror, they would not look or listen; like an angry
demon

Their fear ran round the house, from room to room.
At last their mother led them off to bed.

Allison lit his pipe; forgot it, thinking.
Something more had been released
Than long-necked Punch, nodding and leering still.
As in the ancient casuistry of Eden,
Falsehood, accepted, falsified all truth;
All the old pleasant facts now fell away,
Flimsy as Christmas wrappings; there was the house, now.
Pretty with snows, with candy roofs and sills,
Sparkling and false as the hut in the fairy tale;
As if in a haunted forest shone the tree,
With fruits—pear, apple, plum—all poison-bright.
Outside the wind swept away the Christmas illusion, raising a white
                                                              fog
Where toys like Martians stalked, destroying all.

He thought: how simply terror can enter a house.
The angel, treed, was trembling, that had promised peace.

The Statue

Emblem of fury, caught in immortal storm,
On that quaint-coated back, flung arm, rough arrogant head,
All weathers of all seasons have been shed;
No season, no mortal weather can much harm
A man of metal, whose imperious form
Dazzles, lighting up a century that buried him in its darkness and
                                                    thought him dead.

Absolute devotion to a cause
May turn a man wholly to metal, make his whole action and thought
Into a tall tower of passionate pride; transfix him, rapt as he was
For strangers and questioning children to point out;
No matter, for his faith led him; but those who look back and doubt
Leave for their monument a pillar of salt that the first rain topples
                                                          and thaws.

What if too stern an ecstasy froze the will
And wrought this rigor in the soul at last?
—The mouth a harsh horn, the staring eyeballs still

Struck with their horrid vision, as though peril were never past?
The metal of his courage, though melted down and recast,
Would thunder as cannon, clang as alarum bell.

He stands too fierce for soft skies: rude, violent, half mad;
Only the hurricane and the earthquake show
The cataclysm for which the hero was bred,
The force that shapes defiance, when, although
All heaven's worst wild-fire streams against his brow,
It wreathes but more terrible a garland of fury for the furious head.

At a Military Ceremony

Praise the soldier innocent as his rifle,
Praise him in the splendor of his wounds
More terrible than Sebastian's or Christ's:

Say that flower-like from his blood in the fiery wastes
Tall cities spring, where lights hang thick as dews,
And peace, like perfume from a saint's tomb, wells;

The altar is painful enough, may the victim perish
Ignorant that his gods are sticks and stones
And that this death is death, like any other.

Inscription for the Tomb of Man *

This is the thing that was not born to die,
Though in bronze ploughlands now the bundled grain
Of the last harvest lies, though not again
Shall night-bird question past the heart's reply:
Not though the mower with his sheaf lies down,
Himself an harvest, and in starlit frost
As well borne home, what time the leaves are lost,
The birds evicted, and the night brought on.
Nor shall the hills, nor crest of any king
Found on the wave-worn casement and sunk porch,
Nor marble boy upholding ruined arch
Before a silent town, outlive this thing,
—This dream of earth, this toy, this shape of clay,
That in an hour the wind must bear away.

 * from *Thing of Sorrow: Poems* (1934).

West of Childhood *
for my brother, George Gardner

West of our childhood rote usurps the rites of spring, the wild sweet
season is an act of year. Uniformed robins hop and tweet
in chorus and culls from showgirls of seed catalogues doll up the view,
embellishing our Garden Homes, while Latin shrubs perform on cue.

A child's fierce focused gaze can wholly enter
and instantly become the bold gold center
of a single crocus, a listening child is fused to the sole voice
of that particular inimitable bird whose red choice
breast is robiner than never, a child perceives
the slow resolving of the one bud to the very leaf of leaves.

East of now and years from Illinois the shout of spring out-rang the
dinner bell.
Brother do you remember the walled garden, our dallies in that
ding dong dell
where my fistful of violets mazed the air we moved through and upon
and a swallow of brook skimmed your tabloid sloop to sea and gone?

North of tomorrow your daughter's daughter's ears will ding with
spring, wild
violets will forest in her fist scenting towns of space; and my son's
child
(weddings from this suburb) will, with crocus eyes, flower other
Mays:
That bud will leaf again, that choice bird sing, and paper boats sail
down the robin days.

* This and the following poems are from *West of Childhood: Poems 1950–1965* (1965).

172

The Searchlight
from an anti-aircraft battery

In smug delight we swaggered through the park
and arrogant pressed arm and knee and thigh.
We could not see the others in the dark.
We stopped and peered up at the moonless sky
and at grey bushes and the bristling grass
You in your Sunday suit, I in my pleated gown,
deliberately we stooped (brim-full of grace,
each brandied each rare-steaked) and laid us down.

We lay together in that urban grove
an ocean from the men engaged to die.
As we embraced a distant armoured eye
aroused our dusk with purposed light, a grave
rehearsal for another night. The field
bloomed lovers, dined and blind and target-heeled.

The Sloth

Body very hairy, tenacious of life.
CARL LINNAEUS (*1707–1778*)

Two centuries ago Linnaeus said "noise frightful, tears pitiful" of you,
bungled one. Arm over hairy arm you travel having no heels
to take to on your unsoled feet, no hole to hide in, and no way to
fight.
Doomed to the trees, "good food for many," your one safety is in
flight.

Today the scarce and lonely sloth, obedient prisoner in space,
astonished by perpetual pain looks askingly into my face
and hangs by legs and arms to life inexorably upside down
under branches in the zoo or in the subway under town.

Little Rock Arkansas 1957

Dedicated to the Nine Children

Clasping like bucklers to their bodies, books,
nine children move through blasts of killing looks.
Committed to this battle each child dares,
deliberately, the fusillades of jeers.
Their valor iron in their ironed clothes
they walk politely in their polished shoes
down ambushed halls to classrooms sown with mines
to learn their lesson. Obviously nine's
a carefully calculated number, odd
not even, a suave size that can be add-
ed to, discreetly, later, or culled now
should one child break not bend; or fail to bow
sufficiently his bloody head . . . a rule
to heed, child, be you brave and going to school.

Cowardice

The amputated human hearts pulse in the great glass jars.
As moist and wincing red as pigeon feet, the breathing hearts
Oscillate endlessly in fluid ambiguity,
and isolated, pickle in the brine of phantasy.

The jars will never be unsealed, nor can the heart be joined,
healed, to the breast. For in that vacuum, that fatal void
between the unreal and the real, between the brine and breast
the heart will burst. And we, compassionate, cannot redeem
the prisoned hearts, nor save the crippled men, the fear-oppressed,
who only suffer love within the prism of a dream.

Abraham and Isaac

"Behold the fire and the wood but where is the lamb
for the burnt offering?" said little Isaac trembling.
"God will provide," said Abraham.
      Fathers of Isaacs cease dissembling.
      Will every thicket yield a ram?

Homo Gratia Artis

Ass-eared cross-gartered haloed crowned
Pearl-eyed and coral-boned and drowned
Victim-father son bride-mother
You are Abel and his brother
Eden Persepolis and Hell
Raskolnikoff and Philomel
The lamb the unicorn the goat
The burning shirt and Joseph's coat
The bleeding ear the bled-for nose
The apple mistletoe and rose
You are the coffin and the cock
The pain the talon and the rock.

Driving at Sunset *

Eastward a huddle: silos, knolls are null,
Gummy as an amateur's oil forty.
Eastward all whereabouts all function sunk;
Barns but a hint of geometry in rorschach

Inkling of comfort, slumber. But see that west!
Each maple quivering in its right acre
Wider than day, each leaf a tongue exclaiming
Through spokes of lava light as never at noon:

A Troy-light. Troy-lit Helen, hair unfurled like
Disaster's serene oilsmoke, make us immortal.
Sing us, through wheel's violin-shrill, volley of gravel,
Right heart, right homestead in the imperiling west.

The Weeds

By the hot hedge of August these were nothing,
Were nothing in the faddish trees of May.
But now in January this copper garden
Holds Fête-champêtre day,

Glum mercury under his glassy ladder sulking.
The fields are lacquer of ice.
Only the waist-high straggle of roan weeds
Extravagant and precise:

One like the peacock's tail imitated in brass;
One with its quarter-inch roses, moth-miller hue;
One like a sepia photo of fireworks; one
Pale-blue as twirl of tattoo.

---

* "Driving at Sunset" and the following poem, "The Weeds," are from *Fountain in Kentucky* (1950).

How could they but be all energy, whorling and torque
Who have survived December trumpeting by;
And bent from the pole star seen, night after night,
White-hot constellations warping the sky?

If barometers told time, these endured epochs.
When all the floe loomed verdant, these were there;
Saw the Green Age itself, unthinkable summer—
These fossils vised in the angry quartz of air.

Elevated *

Three stories up the town is Venice: there
The streets' abrupt and windy rivers run
Among the badland brick, the domes of tar,
The mica prairie wheeling in the sun.
On crags of glass the sooty lichen twine;
Flowers of the wash in highland vineyards shine.

Along the banks of tile and metal mushroom
The orange liners of the transit ply.
From bunks of plush the mariners behold
The hollow maelstrom with indifferent eye.
Serene to wreck, they loll and even read,
Their schooner reeling in a sea of speed.

The green pagoda, floating in the tree,
Honors the pauper and the drunk buffoon,
Slow negroes too (the negatives of men)
Wearing their midnight faces even at noon.
All come and throw, like dice, the copper fare,
Win ships of glass and navigate the air

Master the changes of all weather too:
When steeples quaver in the August glow
Or windows in wet April spin like reels
Or when the track's a portico of snow.
Mostly at rung Noël, the frozen star
Hears all night long the heaven-skating car.

* This and the following poem, "City Rain at Midnight," are from *Iron Pastoral*
(1947).

We float an eerie deep, as men that mark
The fabulous water in a keel of glass;
Beneath the bay of rippling window, loom
The tenant's cave and honeycomb crevasse —
Queer grots of mossy rug, crustacea pan,
Framing the sad and seahorse shape of man.

On nights of rain, the captain in the prow
Dares in great dark the iron-charted flood,
Follows a star of harbor green as mint,
Skirting disaster's little eye of blood.
Is fortunate yet, for sudden in the night
Stations arrive like Indias of light.

Exotic foliage on the wooden shore
Fertile with ads: tobacco, rouge, and coke
Finer than flora swarm. Have proper care
From censoring pigeon, friend to lonely folk.
Here girls in jest or desperate or tight
(Like votive wax) their phone and hungers write.

What dreamer hung the hollow sky with ore?
No Merlin he, or caliph in a tale.
Some ne'er-do-well, some boy who liked to draw
Blueprinted first the levitating rail.
Rubbed a right lamp, and saw, when that was done,
A crowded city moving in the sun.

The crazy dream is record and charts time,
Gables the region with a frieze of steel.
Saturn is peeled of credit, on whose ring
Never the flash and thunder of such wheel,
Where no batons of hard momentum flail
Music of acrid iron from the rail.

As princes, wrecked and ragged, long pursued,
Show in some tone the grandeurs of their birth,
So we, who fever on a foreign bed,
Who beg for lust and moulder in sad earth,
Greatness remember, and with viking eye
Storm the ancestral headlands of the sky.

City Rain at Midnight

The rain and neon lock
And the glass machinery moves.
Like wheels of a slow clock
Pools on the sidewalk turn;
In the trolley's ornate grooves,
In the awning, overhead urn,
Forces gather. And then
Unspring and gather again.

Runnels, gentle alarm,
Strum in the cogs of air;
Safe heads on a safe arm
Never will waken for these;
But men who loiter and stare,
Who scuff in the public trees —
Feeling cold ratchets lock,
Shiver, caught in a clock.

Girl Marcher *

Now *Ban The Bomb!* I'm with you, though we fail.
Did *Ban The Arrow! Ban The Fist!* avail?
Still the red lips, ecstatic, cry "Ban! Ban!"
First ban yourself, sweet marcher. Banish man.

Old Philosophy Professor

These pretty students all the years!
The heart too often stumbles: none
But skirt the orchards worth a world.
Paths of the many. And the one.

* This and the two poems following are from *Of Flesh and Bone* (1967).

Poetry Dignitary

He lectures, palms extended on the air,
Much like the pope to bless St. Peter's Square.
Heaps laurel on his bumpy brow benign;
Chants, "Acres of Parnassus, and all mine!"

To Keep Our Metaphysics Warm? *

Time is no runner; we run. Time outstays the
Clocks loping like spiders up granite; like fossils in silica fused.
How the aplomb of old few-worded sundials
Sags, by weather's mere maneuver abused.

Time past, we say. The market of our commerce
Early benighted, calls our night the year's.
Grey skulls (O no Greek steps) grow dead-moon pitted;
Corinthian flies; our doric knee despairs.

Here glimmer north and south shark-patrolled oceans;
In clouds of cloudy Now the ecliptics start.
Though time is our conservative friend, we fail him
Betrayed by our most fed, most petted part,

The camellia curling around, say *better* bone?
Or say: that trellis quite smothered in summer, gaunt
In fall, no season's pleasure. Take my hand
Camellia girl, many many a shade of summer.

Only your fingers (lucky exodus)
Upon this ocean float my sinkable bone.
Through the Acropolis and Forum lead me;
Mock with an impudent lovelock time's milestone.

* from *Fountain in Kentucky.*

To Be in Love *

To be in love
Is to touch things with a lighter hand.

In yourself you stretch, you are well.

You look at things
Through his eyes.
A Cardinal is red.
A sky is blue.
Suddenly you know he knows too.
He is not there but
You know you are tasting together
The winter, or light spring weather.

His hand to take your hand is overmuch.
Too much to bear.

You cannot look in his eyes
Because your pulse must not say
What must not be said.

When he
Shuts a door—
Is not there—
Your arms are water.

And you are free
With a ghastly freedom.

You are the beautiful half
Of a golden hurt.

You remember and covet his mouth,
To touch, to whisper on.

* This and the following poems are from *Selected Poems* (1963).

Oh when to declare
Is certain Death!

Oh when to apprize
Is to mesmerize,

To see fall down, the Column of Gold,
Into the commonest ash.

The Bean Eaters

They eat beans mostly, this old yellow pair.
Dinner is a casual affair.
Plain chipware on a plain and creaking wood,
Tin flatware.

Two who are Mostly Good.
Two who have lived their day,
But keep on putting on their clothes
And putting things away.

And remembering . . .
Remembering, with twinklings and twinges,
As they lean over the beans in their rented back room that is full of
    beads and receipts and dolls and cloths, tobacco crumbs, vases
            and fringes.

The Lovers of the Poor

    arrive. The Ladies from the Ladies' Betterment League
Arrive in the afternoon, the late light slanting
In diluted gold bars across the boulevard brag
Of proud, seamed faces with mercy and murder hinting
Here, there, interrupting, all deep and debonair,
The pink paint on the innocence of fear;
Walk in a gingerly manner up the hall.
Cutting with knives served by their softest care,
Served by their love, so barbarously fair.
Whose mothers taught: You'd better not be cruel!
You had better not throw stones upon the wrens!
Herein they kiss and coddle and assault
Anew and dearly in the innocence

With which they baffle nature. Who are full,
Sleek, tender-clad, fit, fiftyish, a-glow, all
Sweetly abortive, hinting at fat fruit,
Judge it high time that fiftyish fingers felt
Beneath the lovelier planes of enterprise.
To resurrect. To moisten with milky chill.
To be a random hitching-post or plush.
To be, for wet eyes, random and handy hem.
        Their guild is giving money to the poor.
The worthy poor. The very very worthy
And beautiful poor. Perhaps just not too swarthy?
Perhaps just not too dirty nor too dim
Nor—passionate. In truth, what they could wish
Is—something less than derelict or dull.
Not staunch enough to stab, though, gaze for gaze!
God shield them sharply from the beggar-bold!
The noxious needy ones whose battle's bald
Nonetheless for being voiceless, hits one down.
        But it's all so bad! and entirely too much for them.
The stench; the urine, cabbage, and dead beans,
Dead porridges of assorted dusty grains,
The old smoke, *heavy* diapers, and, they're told,
Something called chitterlings. The darkness. Drawn
Darkness, or dirty light. The soil that stirs.
The soil that looks the soil of centuries.
And for that matter the *general* oldness. Old
Wood. Old marble. Old tile. Old old old.
Not homekind Oldness! Not Lake Forest, Glencoe.
Nothing is sturdy, nothing is majestic,
There is no quiet drama, no rubbed glaze, no
Unkillable infirmity of such
A tasteful turn as lately they have left,
Glencoe, Lake Forest, and to which their cars
Must presently restore them. When they're done
With dullards and distortions of this fistic
Patience of the poor and put-upon.
        They've never seen such a make-do-ness as
Newspaper rugs before! In this, this "flat,"
Their hostess is gathering up the oozed, the rich
Rugs of the morning (tattered! the bespattered. . . .)
Readies to spread clean rugs for afternoon.
Here is a scene for you. The Ladies look,
In horror, behind a substantial citizeness

Whose trains clank out across her swollen heart.
Who, arms akimbo, almost fills a door.
All tumbling children, quilts dragged to the floor
And tortured thereover, potato peelings, soft-
Eyed kitten, hunched-up, haggard, to-be-hurt.
     Their League is allotting largesse to the Lost.
But to put their clean, their pretty money, to put
Their money collected from delicate rose-fingers
Tipped with their hundred flawless rose-nails seems . . .
     They own Spode, Lowestoft, candelabra,
Mantels, and hostess gowns, and sunburst clocks,
Turtle soup, Chippendale, red satin "hangings,"
Aubussons and Hattie Carnegie. They Winter
In Palm Beach; cross the Water in June; attend,
When suitable, the nice Art Institute;
Buy the right books in the best bindings; saunter
On Michigan, Easter mornings, in sun or wind.
Oh Squalor! This sick four-story hulk, this fibre
With fissures everywhere! Why, what are bringings
Of loathe-love largesse? What shall peril hungers
So old old, what shall flatter the desolate?
Tin can, blocked fire escape and chitterling
And swaggering seeking youth and the puzzled wreckage
Of the middle passage, and urine and stale shames
And, again, the porridges of the underslung
And children children children. Heavens! That
Was a rat, surely, off there, in the shadows? Long
And long-tailed? Gray? The Ladies from the Ladies'
Betterment League agree it will be better
To achieve the outer air that rights and steadies,
To hie to a house that does not holler, to ring
Bells elsetime, better presently to cater
To no more Possibilities, to get
Away. Perhaps the money can be posted.
Perhaps they two may choose another Slum!
Some serious sooty half-unhappy home! —
Where loathe-love likelier may be invested.
     Keeping their scented bodies in the center
Of the hall as they walk down the hysterical hall,
They allow their lovely skirts to graze no wall,
Are off at what they manage of a canter,
And, resuming all the clues of what they were,
Try to avoid inhaling the laden air.

Riders to the Blood-Red Wrath

My proper prudence toward his proper probe
Astonished their ancestral seemliness.
It was a not-nice risk, a wrought risk, was
An indelicate risk, they thought. And an excess.
Howas I handled my discordances
And prides and apoplectic ice, howas
I reined my charger, channeled the fit fume
Of his most splendid honorable jazz
Escaped the closing and averted sight
Waiving all witness except of rotted flowers
Framed in maimed velvet. That mad demi-art
Of ancient and irrevocable hours.
Waiving all witness except of dimnesses
From which extrude beloved and pennant arms
Of a renegade death impatient at his shrine
And keen to share the gases of his charms.
They veer to vintage. Careening from tomorrows.
They loot Last Night. They hug old graves, root up
Decomposition, warm it with a kiss.

The National Anthem vampires at the blood.
I am a uniform. Not brusque. I bray
Through blur and blunder in a little voice!
This is a tender grandeur, a tied fray!
Under macabres, stratagem and fair
Fine smiles upon the face of holocaust,
My scream! unedited, unfrivolous.
My laboring unlatched braid of heat and frost.
I hurt. I keep that scream in at what pain:
At what repeal of salvage and eclipse.
Army unhonored, meriting the gold, I
Have sewn my guns inside my burning lips.

Did they detect my parleys and replies?
My Revolution pushed his twin the mare,
The she-thing with the soft eyes that conspire
To lull off men, before him everywhere.
Perhaps they could not see what wheedling bent
Her various heart in mottles of submission

And sent her into a firm skirmish which
Has tickled out the enemy's sedition.

They do not see how deftly I endure.
Deep down the whirlwind of good rage I store
Commemorations in an utter thrall.
Although I need not eat them any more.

I remember kings.
A blossoming palace. Silver, Ivory.
The conventional wealth of stalking Africa.
All bright, all Bestial. Snarling marvelously.

I remember my right to roughly run and roar.
My right to raid the sun, consult the moon.
Nod to my princesses or split them open,
To flay my lions, eat blood with a spoon.
You never saw such running and such roaring! —
Nor heard a burgeoning heart so craze and pound! —
Nor sprang to such a happy rape of heaven!
Nor sanctioned such a kinship with the ground!

And I remember blazing dementias
Aboard such trade as maddens any man.
. . . The mate and captain fragrantly reviewed
The fragrant hold and presently began
Their retching rampage among their luminous
Black pudding, among the guttural chained slime:
Half fainting from their love affair with fetors
That pledged a haughty allegiance for all time.

I recollect the latter lease and lash
And labor that defiled the bone, that thinned
My blood and blood-line. All my climate my
Foster designers designed and diciplined.

But my detention and my massive stain,
And my distortion and my Calvary
I grind into a little light lorgnette
Most sly: to read man's inhumanity.
And I remark my Matter is not all.
Man's chopped in China, in India indented.

From Israel what's Arab is resented.
Europe candies custody and war.

Behind my exposé
I formalize my pity: "I shall cite,
Star, and esteem all that which is of woman,
Human and hardly human."

Democracy and Christianity
Recommence with me.

And I ride ride I ride on to the end—
Where glowers my continuing Calvary.
I,
My fellows, and those canny consorts of
Our spread hands in this contretemps-for-love
Ride into wrath, wraith and menagerie

To fail, to flourish, to wither or to win.
We lurch, distribute, we extend, begin.

A Roof-top, Late August *

How they creep now, slowly from the jungle of stars,
The uncertain grey shapes, where you lie suspended,
Their heads down, like inexorable dancers knowing
More than the music knows, untouched and far
From any music, strangers to what they hear.
They move now in their doing or undoing
Strong with the whole past in them distended,
Above your small clear tentative of air.

You would sleep now, drawing your perilous bed
On the narrow pronoun *I* held undefended
Between fierce love and fiercer thought. The darkness
Swollen with all the rumors of the glade
Waits in a breathing circle. Nothing is dead
That cannot now return bright-eyed and heartless
To dance around your dreams or madden the slender
Needle whereby this moment's thought is weighed.

And it weeps now, your moment bends and weeps.
All that has lived and died in you can lend it
Nothing but heavy tears. And you must study
An undissolving alphabet to keep,
In the dim landscape of these liquid shapes
And the flooding fever in the mind and body,
The legend of your consciousness extended
Steep as a tree-house, in a night more steep.

Lovers That Leave

Lovers that leave take nothing in division:
No merchant's ledgering will calculate
A balance of this wealth; no lawyer's reason.
They leave as paupers all their joint estate.

* This and the two poems following are from *The Travelers* (1949).

Lovers that lived warm in a warmth all winter
Go cold into the cold with cold desire.
Gross and divided now, how shall they kindle
Their faggots from that chaste and simple fire?

They are returned to selves: wanting each other,
They are two wants; two sighs, although they burst.
Let them bruise mouth on mouth, cleaving together:
They cannot drink. They taste only their thirst.

Each will regained, they wander undirected;
Each with resistance proved now loiters where
No thought of rule and no defense constructed
A clear republic fortressed of bright air.

Abstraction

A straight line and a curve beside it: "All
Verticals are men." Their shapes are what they cry.
The curve waits like a mother or the slowly
Entombing earth. Sebastian to its sky,
Shall this line stand though the invisible
Vectors transfix its side? The decimals
Only postpone the curving destiny
Toward which the logarithms slide and fall.

Toward which all space, as Einstein dreamed;
Toward which the myth coiled in our algebras
And three numbers that sang the Parthenon
Into a solid. Mark the splendid pause
Before this line plunges to meet its love
Where love is whirled with death. This vertical
Is motion as one moment and recalled
Erect with risk, electric with its law.

My Mother's Portrait *

Your world is under glass. What storms I can remember now
Are faëry. My own child's-voice is muted
As in a far world on a dim music floated
I hear it speak to you.

* This and the two poems following are from *A Sky of Late Summer* (1963).

I have been away, and now I sit again where your eyes command
The world of their peace, not asking or telling
Of any season but the one beyond failing
Enclosed forever in your hands.

It rains. I am troubled. And I beg as I have always done,
Stranger to stranger, always across the thousand
Fears of the night and in all my world's strange houses,
Pray for your son.

The Net

For my students at the University of Chicago, 1947–1954

A wide net I needed
When that room leapt with words
Here to the left, and there
Where I almost missed. Or the words
Were all the net there was:
The walls
Faded, the room
Lithe as a net
Stirred, a wide low
Shimmering. It was
Such poor thread as we had,
Tied upon thread:
Speech crossed on speech
Joined and secured
Now gathering speech
The rich weight glowing.

Hold now, hold,
I had to shout each time,
This that is all our doing,
This that we owe one another,
Hans, Yale, James,
Bunny in her bright tears,
Emrich, Minda Rae,
And the student always called
Sir, Stray
Visitor from some
Remote class, with terms

Yet more remote, now
Held and holding
Forever with us, this
Vivid morning:
Hold, hold now
(I cry still
In a stillness)
This, such as it is,
That we have made, all of us,
And gather
With what we made.

Sit Now, Quietly

Sit now, quietly, while the last
Phantoms diminish and dissolve, and the
Lost voices droop upon their argument.
Your silence will forgive all argument,
The sanctuary of your hands hold fast
The real from unreal, hold the free.

Look now, openly, with the clear
Courtesy of your eyes: a closure draws
Its peace upon the compass of your sight.
O when at last you sleep, I beg you close
In your closed eyes my world, and safely bear
The world to morning within your good night.

On Finding a Bird's Bones in the Woods *

Even Einstein, gazing
at the slender ribs of the worlds,
examining and praising
the cool and tranquil core
under the boil and burning
of faith and metaphor—
even he, unlearning
the bag and baggage of notion,
must have kept some shred
in which to clothe that shape,
as we who cannot escape
imagination, swaddle
this tiny world of bone
in all that we have known
of sound and motion.

Cicadas

Always in unison, they are
the rapt voice of silence,

so singleminded I cannot tell
if the sound is rich or thin,

cannot tell even if it is sound,
the high, sustained note

which gives to a summer field
involved with the sun at noon

a stillness as palpable
as smoke and mildew,

* This and the following poems, unless otherwise indicated, are from *Dependencies* (1965).

know only: when they are gone
one scrubbed autumn day

after the clean sweep
of the bright, acrid season,

what remains is a clearing of rest,
of balance and attention

but not the second skin,
hot and close, of silence.

Sunday Fishing

Another minor jungle has been cleared,
tenuous lattices of light and shade
bulldozed from memory, shy things expelled
toward a stop-gap refuge, some last ditch
of secrecy, so we may park and pay
for public leisure under blasts of sun
in a brand-new, two-acre wonderland
where red and yellow candy wrappers toss
in the displeasure of a dirty wind.

Even the bite is fixed. The trout that stock
the baby blue of these invented streams
know better than to try and get away;
they shame us by compliance, come in droves
as if to mock the old prerogatives
which used to let us gamble on our luck
and test our patience under willow trees
while watching all the humors of the sky —
in on the game, these creatures gulp and die.

Tires spin and screech, as bright, insensate fins
threaten each other in their push to church
along the highway, a few feet from us:
what fool thought he could give us Paradise
with gravel walks and whittled redwood signs
and paid-for guarantees? Already flawed,
this garden galls what innocence we have —
let's throw the rainbows back and take a chance
along some godforsaken country creek.

Suspension Bridge: Twilight

The smoking, rusting beast
—our green ankylosaurus—

refines itself to a hum
between these silver strands

hammered for an imagined
woman's white-knuckled wrist

—a lady's rather, small,
slenderly old-fashioned,

the wrist of one who delights
in such sherbet sunsets

as this one in raspberry, filched
from a romance. Yet we bump

ashore in another part
of the land, and looking back

see her stand unbroken,
swaying only a little

as if she felt, too late,
the weight of our bon voyage.

The People at the Party

They are like tightrope walkers, unable to fall
from the precise thread of their making,
having achieved the most delicate of all
balances of the brain, which is forsaking

joy on the one hand, and on the other, terror;
holding themselves exquisitely aloof
from the contingencies of love and error,
they dare nothing, are wholly removed

by the will not to suffer, from us who do.
Ah, but they are precariously perched
on their rope of detachment. Who
can be sure someone improperly coached

won't say the wrong word or turn back
the cruel joke with a human response?
That the only girl not in serpent black
will keep her distance? There is always a chance

someone careless or young will unsettle the cable,
bring on the vertigo and set them reeling
toward the sheer drop, toward the unstable
inexorable wilderness of feeling.

Ecology: The Lion

Let me illustrate by way of example
from history, from the last war:
when the city burned that day, that night,
those many days and nights, the flames
finally bit through the bars of his cage
and set him free. He was wary of freedom
at first, of its charred, black taste. But the fire
drove him out of the zoo and eastward
and his confidence grew in the burned-out streets
where children stuck to the boiling asphalt;
heat urged his soles like the native heat
of his rampant days, and when he reached
the river, spurred by sounds of panic
breaking through leafage of smoke,
he felt easy enough to stand still
and savor the scent of catastrophe
that welcomed him like a greeting from home.

The Lonesome Dream

In the America of the dream
the first rise of the moon
swings free of the ocean,
and she reigns in her shining flesh
over a good, great valley
of plumed, untrampled grasses
and beasts with solemn eyes,
of lovers infallibly pitched
in their ascendant phase.

In this America, death
is virginal also, roaming
the good, great valley
in his huge boots, his shadow
steady and lean, his pistol
silver, his greeting clear
and courteous as a stranger's
who looks for another, a mind
to share his peaceable evenings.

Dreaming, we are another
race than the one which wakes
in the cold sweat of fear,
fires wild shots at death,
builds slippery towers of glass
to head him off, waylays him
with alcohol traps, rides him down
in the haunts of thought and thighs,
our teetering ghost towns.

Dreaming, we are the mad
who swear by the blood of trees
and speak with the tongues of streams
through props of steel and sawdust;
a colony of souls
ravaged by visions, bound
to some wild, secret cove
not yet possessed, a place
still innocent of us.

The Gift of Fire *

In memory of Norman Morrison, who burned himself to
death in front of the Pentagon on November 2, 1965

In a time of damnation
when the world needed a Savior,
when the dead gathered routinely,
comic-strip flat and blurred,

he took the god at his promise
and set himself on fire,
skin, brain, sex, smile

so we should see, really see
by that unbearable light
the flower of the single face,
the intricate moth of consciousness:

but he lived in the land of the one-eyed
where the blind is king.

* from *Poetry: A Magazine of Verse,* July, 1967.

In Cities *

There are many underground things
in cities, things like sewers,
that run for miles, lengths
and widths, across cities,
under all. Then there are
the basements of large stores,
houses and hotels, and often
these basements run for twenty feet
and more out, around the buildings;
and coal, garbage and all kinds
of food are sent up and down into
the basements, or out, from the side-
walks and the alleys and streets,
by chutes, corrugated elevator-
stands, iron platforms, sewertops
. . . round, rectangular or square.

And these metal things in the sidewalks,
streets, are always rather warm;
and in the winter, to comfort
and unbitter their sittings,
haunches and tails, and to avoid
the asphalt ice and cold, cats
and dogs, stray squirrels
and so forth, come at night
and from miles around, rest
and together partake.
                    And from some
distances, they and their live optic
green, brown congregations of eyes
appear as islands, still yellow
large, oval, gray or opalesque.
And no dog bites no cat, nor squirrel,

* This and the two poems following are from *Kissing the Dancer and Other Poems* (1964).

and all is quiet, idle, until the sun
comes up and chases them
out of the night, off the warmth
and good of the sewers to their parts
and tails. Then without a look
at the sun, itself, they run, trot
walking, no, no business into the snow.

Snow

The snow began to fall and, pleased
With its falling, and the thick
Light effect of itself, blackwhite
Against the summer, frozen
Town, it gathered in momentum
Independent of the wind
And let itself tumble, with a
Quick, sensual uncontrol . . .

Like some unmiraculous *white*
Of a woman, stripped and gathered
Into the lightest freezings
Of herself
          —pleased by her being
And the thick of herself, as such,
Upon the dead spread of streets, steeples
And the noon hour of the night.

All the Mornings

All the mornings, always pennies
Of my life.
Nickels, dimes
      shafts of light, clouds
Have begun
      over things—an alley,
Bushes, pawnshops,
          people.

It is a part of fish, rent-
    stench
Curtain smells,
        tenements
    to be three, four
Five flights above the street,
Over what in the good years
Of a good war one falls on
    now and then,
        dreams on, dies, a park.

All the evenings, always
        streetlights
Buildings, trees
    sculptured out of stone
      Moon
Nickels, dimes
    I'm falling,
      slowly
Quite slowly, now, down
Into the shafts of light.

American Heritage *

This, O my stomach, is a painting
Of the Civil War. Look—Antietam.
All over there are dead,
Noble Northern, Noble Southern, dead.
One, no, no, several wear beards:
They are all General Ulysses S. Grant beards,
Noble, truly noble beards.
The Union side, O my soul, see them!
All, all of them noble,
All, all of them waving.
Resembling, bearing the name
Walt Whitman. They are all on horseback,
All with maps and swords, banners
And copies of last Sunday's
New York *Times* Book Review;
Watching through binoculars,
Writing letters, keeping journals,
Reading *Leaves of Grass* . . .

* from *The Thousand-Year-Old Fiancée* (1965).

And there is Barbara Frietchie.
Hi, Barbara. Barbara's pregnant.
She is soon to be the mother
Of Abraham Lincoln, Dr. Oliver Wendell Holmes
And Carl Sandburg.
This is an historical moment;
Very historical. You can feel it
And read about it, too
(And General Stonewall Jackson,
Clare Boothe Luce, Robert E. Lee
    and many others),
In *American Heritage*
Edited by Bruce Catton,
With whose kind permission
I herewith reprint this painting.

.   .   .   .

Song: "There's No War Like Civil War"
    O the Civil War's
    The only war,
    The only war, the only war;
    The finest war,
    Yes, the noblest most unforeign war,
    The finest only noblest most
    Unforeign war
    That ever I did see.
                    (*Chorus, etc.*)

Chicago Elegy *

In a six-horse carriage painted pickle-green
     the Infanta Eulalia
  at last rolls up the drive, and stomps
     into the gothic castle
Potter Palmer'd built of granite:
to pout there on a plump blue punjab rug
     that covers her settee.
  Despite the cario windowpanes,
     the summer night seeps in.
The city reeks of butchered pigs and sheep.

But Long John Wentworth, pulling at a stogy,
     sprawls on a drygoods box,
  spits, and drawls to the reporters:
     "Boys, you got it plum
     assbackward: I didn't set next to
the Prince of Wales; the Prince set next to me."
     A prairie dog, the harvest
  moon, now curls its paws and naps
     among the nettles here
in this vacant lot where Mrs. Potter Palmer,

from her tower, heard the flocks of ghosts
     of Pottawottomies
  mourning in the prairie grass
     around Fort Dearborn's pinewood
palisade. Those traffic lights
twitching along the Outer Drive, might be
     the tomahawks, and cattail
  torches that danced a witches' sabbath
     in the ashes of the Fort.
Or like the lantern sparks licking from

* from *The Prairies Schooner*, Fall, 1957.

O'Leary's loft, they jerk and rampage through
    the old frame stores and stables.
  But like a young grass widow, Chicago
    sits solitary only
long enough to catch her breath.
With fist of concrete, steel, pigiron, stone,
    with mind of birds flown home
  in April, Louis Sullivan
    rams into the soil
the long roots of the Auditorium:

as if to cry into the teeth of lake,
    sand-dune and prairie winds,
  the old gods of this land. And yet,
    along your river banks,
  Chicago, I have never seen
a pair of strolling laughing lovers kiss.
    To you the spectacle
  of Rome or Athens moping over
    a heap of windworn stones,
is wasted time and money down the drain.
Yet let the whole shebang, lock, stock and barrel,
    collapse next Saturday,
  by Monday you'll have brushed the dust
    and rubble off, and stuck
  new structures up. For when the sun
at dawn explodes to scatter over Lake Shore Drive,
    Mies van der Rohe's glass hands
  catch at the gulls, the bits and spray,
    juggle them till night,
then pitch back on the lake a 1,000,000 lights.

Mother *

If I seem to patronize and always limit what I say
        to the clichés of affection, mother,
    and never give a good goddamn what you are doing:
            but boast instead
        how I will rake $10,000 in this year;
and with crude, belligerent hints, propped by "proofs"
        from analysis and common sense,
                throw my sex life in your face;
        and if I never kiss you any more

and break our Tuesday dinner dates too often:
        it is because I can still remember
    sprawling on your bed, reciting the litany
            of the Virgin Mary with you,
                even after I'd begun to shave.
And can remember temper tantrums, pulverizing your bedroom mirror
        with a bottle of perfume; or prying in
                your dresser drawers, exploring
        for blue brassieres; or gnawing nails to nubs

or getting stoned drunk when you dated after father died.
        This morning, mother, I saw an alley cat
    gently flop to rub its spine against the fountain
            in pintsized Goudy park
        a block from the Ambassador Hotel.
Two days ago, a batch of pigeons scrimmaged in the grass
        to peck stale crumbs scattered from
                a Wedgewood plate by one of those
        horsey-looking ladies who live on Astor Street.

Today, the pigeons roosting in the sycamore above,
        cat nonchalantly ambling under.
    Suddenly cat zips up the trunk of the tree and
            with a roundhouse swipe
        almost claws a pigeon as it bolts;
then dazed, dangles, and with a moist tongue mops its paw;
        snakes down the trunk, slips, rakes
                at a batch of leaves, misses,
        tumbles six feet down; but balloons its body

* from *The Paris Review,* Spring–Summer, 1965.

to land without a scratch. Then stalks agilely away,
    without a look, into the shrubbery.
  You talk a lot about religion now.
      Remember, mother, Mary,
    our maid for Connemara, that afternoon,
snow gouging against the windowpane, when she bawled but
    stubbornly refused to make the bed
      on which your best friend
    and her Monseignor had just thrashed about,

making a mess of it. Even now, after I have made it
    with one woman or another,
  a line from out old litany goes jagging through my head—
      "Tower of Ivory: pray for us.
  House of Gold: pray for us. Mother most pure:
pray for us. Mother Undefiled: pray for us. Pray for us.
  Virgin most pure: pray for us. Pray.
      Holy Mary, mother of God,
    pray for us sinners now and at the hour

of our death. Amen." Nothing colder than this snow
    of memory. How many years
  did I drag myself out to the Dominicans to bitch
      with them about the Church,
    asking for proof my body was corrupt?
Still fat Aquinas put his finger on it when he insisted
  in his *Summa* that incest was actually infantile:
      an avarice of the emotions.
    He knew the heart for the famished cat it is.

Oriental Pastoral:

OLD SCHOLARS, A BIRD, A PLUMTREE [*]

Feathers turning to mist, the thin blue heron
    Imperceptibly glides by a plumtree
And up the hold mountain. Or have you come
    To sit on a mat beside old scholars,
    And from their bamboo porch to watch
How a blue autumn afternoon alters
    Rock, pool and orchid-plot
Till half-dream is their garden's symmetry?

  * from the *Western Review*, Spring, 1957.

Then, in a dream, the winesour plumtree
    Stirs and blossoms in the snow;
What matter now if once you thought
    That goat-path winding on the mountain,
    That's only taken by the few,
Had to be climbed? One day, they say,
    A scholar brought a proverb back:
You only need so much of sun

    As fingers can close around and burn,
In one blue afternoon. And this:
    Soul like the bird is almost mist.

Bombardier *

Coming out of the station he expected
To bump into the cripple who had clomped,
Bright pencils trailing, across his dreams

For fifteen years. Before setting out
He was ready to offer both his legs,
His arms, his sleepless eyes. But it seemed

There was no need: it looked a healthy town,
The people gay, the new streets dancing
In the famous light. Even the War Museum

With its photos of the blast, the well-mapped
Rubble, the strips of blackened skin,
Moved one momentarily. After all,

From the window one could watch picnickers
Plying chopsticks as before, the children
Bombing carp with rice-balls. Finding not

What he had feared, he went home cured at last.
Yet minutes after getting back in bed
A wood leg started clomping, a thousand

Eyes leapt wild, and once again he hurtled
Down a road paved white with flesh. On waking
He knew he had gone too late to the wrong

Town, and that until his own legs numbed
And eyes went dim with age, somewhere
A fire would burn that no slow tears could quench.

* the first of three poems of "Return to Hiroshima" in the "East" section of
Stryk's *Notes for a Guidebook* (1965).

A Sheaf for Chicago *

Something queer and terrifying about Chicago: one of the
strange "centres" of the earth . . .
                    D. H. LAWRENCE TO HARRIET MONROE

I. PROEM

Always when we speak of you, we call you
Human. You are not. Nor are you any
Of the things we say: queer, terrifying.

It is the tightness of the mind that would
Confine you. No more strange than Paris
Is gay, you exist by your own laws,

Which to the millions that call you theirs,
Suffice, serve the old gargantuan needs.
Heaped as if just risen — streaming, unsmirched —

From seethings far below, you accept all.
By land, air, sea they come, certain to find
You home. For those you've once possessed, there's no

Escaping: always revealed in small
Particulars — a bar, a corner — you
Reappear complete. Even as I address

You, seeing your vastness in alleyways
And lots that fester Woodlawn, I have
A sense of islands all around, made one

By sea that feeds and spoils yet is a thing
Apart. You are that sea. And home: have
Stamped me yours for keeps, will claim me when,

Last chances spent, I wrap it up for good.
You are three million things, and each is true.
But always home. More so and more deeply

---

* "A Sheaf for Chicago," from which poems IV, VI, VII, and VIII have here
been omitted, constitutes the "Heartland" section of *Notes for a Guidebook.*

Than the sum of antheaps we have made of
You, reenter every night to dream you
Something stone can never be. And met

However far away, two that call you
Home, feel beyond the reach of words to tell
Like brothers who must never part again.

II. A CHILD IN THE CITY

In a vacant lot behind a body shop
I rooted for your heart, O city,
The truth that was a hambone in your slop.

Your revelations came as thick as bees,
With stings as smarting, wings as loud,
And I recall those towering summer days

We gathered fenders, axles, blasted hoods
To build Cockaigne and Never-never Land,
Then beat for dragons in the oily weeds.

That cindered lot and twisted auto mound,
That realm to be defended with the blood,
Became as New Year swung around,

A scene of holocaust, where pile on pile
Of Christmas trees would char the heavens
And robe us demon-wild and genie-tall

To swirl the hell of 63rd Place
Our curses whirring by your roofs,
Our hooves a-clatter on your face.

III. THE BALLOON
(*To Auguste Piccard, his day at Soldier Field*)

As you readied the balloon, tugging
At the ropes, I grabbed my father's hand.
Around us in stone tiers the others

Began to hold their breath. I watched my
Father mostly, thinking him very
Brave for toying with his pipe. Then when

You filled the giant sack with heated
Air and, waving, climbed into the
Gondola with a bunch of roses

Thrust at you, I freed my hand, cheered
And started clapping. I caught your eye,
You smiled, then left the ground. The people

Filed for exits when, twisting in
The wind, you veered above the lake, a
Pin against a thundercloud. But I

Refused to budge. My father stooped to
Beat me and cracked his precious briar
On the stone. And still I wouldn't leave.

He called me a young fool and dragged me,
Bawling, to the streetcar. But I couldn't
Stop watching you. I stayed up all that night,

Soaring ever higher on your star,
Through tunneled clouds and air so blue
I saw blue spots for hours. In the morning

My father laughed and said you came back down.
I didn't believe him then, and never will.
I told him I was glad he broke his pipe.

V. MESTROVIC'S INDIANS

(*Equestrian statues, Michigan Avenue*)

With bare heels sharp as spurs
They kick the bronze flanks of
    The horses.

But what sane beast would brave
A river wild as this, choked
    As it is

With jagged tin and all
That snarling rubber? And
    Ford to where?

Along the other bank, while the
Great arms pointing with their
    Manes Convulse

In anger, the merchants
Dangle strings of gewgaws
    In the sun.

But no mere hoof was meant
For plunging here, and why, the
    Horses seem

To ask, would even redskins
Climb a shore where not one
    Grassblade springs?

IX. THE NEIGHBORHOOD

Long away, I find it pure
Exotic; no matter that they roll
The sidewalks up at ten and boys

Want height to leap for basketballs;
It is a place, and there are corners
Where one does what one would do.

Come back, I find the expected
Changes: shabby streets grown shabbier,
The mob all scattered, old girl friends

Losing more of what's been lost,
The supermarts turned up like sows
To give the brood of grunters suck,

And Mother, like a thickening tree
Whose roots work deeper as the woodman
Nears, spread over all, the wind which sweeps

Across her whispering "Stay On."
Two weeks of that, and there are
Other whispers that I heed.

The train pulls in and I descend,
To mount before it pulls away.
Goodby Mother, goodby! I'm off

Again to Someplace Else, where
Chafing together once a month
The strangers sit and write sweet letters home.

Words on a Windy Day *

Airing out the clothes,
    The odor of mothballs
        Driving me inside,
I watch in wonder
    As the wind fills
        Trouserlegs and sweaters,

Whips them light and dark.
    In that frayed coat
        I courted her a year,
In that old jacket
    Married her, then brushed
        Her tears off with a sleeve.

The wind blows through them,
    Tosses them about,
        These mildewed ghosts of love
That life, for lack of something
    Simple as a clothespin,
        Let fall, one by one.

* from the "West" section of *Notes for a Guidebook*.

Travel Poster *

Appalled by unaccustomed beauty,
And yet unable to move, I stand outside,
Strangeness always inexplicable: a sea
All blue, all white-boated; a gentle tide
Leading the eye to green, casual valleys.
But mountains, too: multi-peaked and scaled
(Of course) by smiling hikers. Ah, what worlds
Of love seem possible! Chateaus, Swiss-railed,
Bulge with aggressive girls; some waving —
Their red-lipped smiles and stretched-full blouses
Proving beyond a doubt they're saving
Themselves for me alone; their available houses
Crowded with beds and mothers who don't even care . . .

Odd of the airlines to assume they can fly me there.

The Crippled Girl

Stretched by the darkness and broken by light,
She woke to find the world all clever arms
And legs — bodies that had, somehow, slipped right
By; unsleeping ones; possessed, no doubt, of charms.
But, invariably kind, these wise ones bundled up
Their button-less shirts and raveled sweaters;
Placed them on her table, next to the cup
Containing thimbles, pin cushion, and threaded needles.
She thanked them, and, despite protests, wheeled
Her chair to the stove, offering tea in
Cracked china.
                    Later, the money sealed
Away, she drank herself to sleep with gin
And dreamed through the night as the bed grew soft
That by staring at people their legs fell off.

* This and the two poems following are from *Poem for a Ten Pound Sailfish and Other Sonnets* (1963).

The Dog Cemetery

The bodies of birds are more fleet:
Left to their own disasters, their wings
Serve well enough for shrouds; to compete
For ground too unseemly, among other things.

But, dropped to a rug from strenuous wagging,
Or tripped by a toy not quite retrieved,
A suitable box is found; shovels soon digging.
The wishes unknown of the late deceased.

Despite a noticeable lack of any
Mourners (perhaps the rain?), it all goes well:
No mess; the stone rather nice for the money;
And, most importantly, no beastly smell.

Shut so tight, no trail leads anywhere;
And no one feeds him but the unkind air.

Holiday *

The black hulks of passing box cars
Let slip through a vertical flash of
Light. Another man, in another car,
Waits on the other side, idle, too.

It is all a part of the same thing:
Sending résumés to the wrong box
Number, forgetting your wife's birthday,
Being unhappy on all the happy days.

* from *The Chicago Review*, Vol. 17 (1964), Nos. 2/3.

Derricks *

Rolling away from Chicago
One drizzly, early morning
Aboard the Rock Island Line's
Peoria Rocket,
I saw above the grey buildings
Four bright-orange derricks
Affably nodding and deferring
To each other;
A warm, aloof, quiet conversation
Of intricate cables and steel struts.

I slid right by,
Under all that metal talk,
Leaving just two shiny rails
To mark my passing.

Northern Indiana, Sunday Afternoon
for Dave

When we finally curled off the Ohio Turnpike,
Weary of all that hot, never-ending stretch
Of cars, grim tourists, the terrible sameness
Of gas, food and postcard service plazas,

And rolled with gratefulness through Indiana's
Fields and towns on U. S. 20, we thought our trip's
Length was, at last, worth it: The Angola courthouse,
The lakes at LaGrange, histories of places like Howe.

But then, as always, the Midwest turned two faces
To even native, resident (and adoring) sons:
The tiny bars were as dry as the large fields.
Whatever our great elation with corn's green progress,

Or wheat's golden, blowing color, man does not live
By sight alone. And so, silently, almost furtively,
We deserted that fertile land and drove straight
North into Michigan. And found in ancient Sturgis

* This and the three poems following are from *Ups and Downs of a Third Baseman* (1963).

Enough cold beer to drown us both. Which almost
Happened, until fond thoughts of dark-haired wives
(And another kind of desire) settled us once more
In your forty miles per hour (but loyal) Simca.

After Chicago claimed us, thoughts of Indiana
So dominated we parted with barely one goodbye.

Poet as Trumpet Player

> *"Poets almost remind me of trumpeters with their profes-
> sional tricks!"*
>
> MOZART, *letter to his father, 1781*

Slipping the horn from my lips,
I gaze expectantly around;
Concerned (like any other vaudevillean)
For applause—at least, some sound

Of recognition. (There're days
When I'd gladly settle
For razzberries.) Does one eventually
Get over this? I fondle

The valves, each one containing
Those precious drops of oil
To smooth the way; to make us think
It's somehow easy to foil

Those anthological roadblocks:
Catullus, Yeats, Villon, Rilke, Dryden—
Try it (in your spare time),
Try leap-frogging them!

Never mind. My repertoire
Is limited, but choice. Listen, here's one
They loved in (where was it?),
Oh well—hey, wait, I'm not done. . . .

The First Death

After the first death, there is no other.
DYLAN THOMAS

The first of us to go, he went so silently
We always somehow felt we'd round a corner
One school-less day and spot that unmanageable
Ruff of hair, that inevitable stoop of shoulder.

We felt most the silence of his life's going.
The violent clash and loss to death we knew
And expected. It was, after all, the war years —
And films every long saturday afternoon

Meant whole hours of ships sliding down
To wet and suffocating deaths; of planes
Spiralling down from skies, trailing the smoke
We knew to be death's consuming flames.

But this other death, this other quiet death,
Crept into dreams that never felt the restless
Shock of war, nor gave a single waking thought
To all the black and white newsprint deaths.

INDEX OF FIRST LINES

INDEX OF POEM TITLES

INDEX OF FIRST LINES

INDEX OF POEM TITLES

225

MEN *of* ZEAL